John Hooper

John Hooper

Pete Sullivan

EP BOOKS
Faverdale North
Darlington
DL3 0PH, England

www.epbooks.org
sales@epbooks.org

EP BOOKS are distributed in the USA by:
JPL Fulfillment
3741 Linden Avenue Southeast,
Grand Rapids, MI 49548.

E-mail: sales@jplfulfillment.com
Tel: 877.683.6935

The right of Pete Sullivan as author of this work has been asserted by him in accordance with the Copyright Designs and Patents Act 1993.

First published 2004 by Country Books, ISBN 978–1–872597–01–0

First EP Books edition published 2014

ISBN: 978–1–78397–009–4

British Library Cataloguing in Publication Data available

For Catherine

Contents

Timeline

	Marriage of John Hooper and Anna de Tserclas at Basle
1548	Rachel Hooper baptized at Zurich by Bullinger
1549	Hooper and family return to England
1550	Hooper preaches Lenten sermons at Court
1551	Hooper consecrated Bishop of Gloucester
1552	Hooper also consecrated Bishop of Worcester
1553	Death of Edward VI and accession of Mary I
1554	Hooper imprisoned in the Fleet
	England formally reconciled to the Church of Rome
1555	Hooper burnt at the stake
1558	Death of Mary I and accession of Elizabeth I

Acknowledgements

Thanks to: Jo Turner for her patience in typing and re-typing the original manuscript; Staff at Churchdown Library, Gloucester Local Studies Library, Gloucester Central Library and Gloucester City Museum and Folk Museum; friends and family who read the manuscript at various stages over the three years of writing this book; The Bishop of Gloucester, the Rt Revd Michael Perham; Antony Wilson at York Coins, Andy Johnson at Logaston Press; The Rev. Iain Murray at The Banner of Truth Trust.

Special thanks to my parents who encouraged my love of books and history and to Gemma, Jodie and Harvey, without whom …

While I am grateful for the advice and encouragement of many people, any errors or misconceptions are entirely my own responsibility.

Illustrations

Front Cover: Portait of Bishop Hooper © Gloucester City Museum and Art Gallery

Back cover: Photograph of the Hooper Monument by the author © Pete Sullivan.

Page 10. Portait of Bishop Hooper © Gloucester City Museum and Art Gallery.

Page 82. Portrait of Ioannes Hooperus © Gloucester City Museum and Art Gallery.

Page 83. Photograph of St Mary's Gateway by the author © Pete Sullivan.

Page 84. Photograph of Gloucester Folk Museum by the author © Pete Sullivan.

Page 84. Philip and Mary Coin courtesy of Antony Wilson at York Coins. www.yorkcoins.com

Page 85. Photographs of the Hooper Monument by the author © Pete Sullivan.

Page 86. The Burning of Master Hooper, Bishop of Gloucester from John Foxe's *Acts and Monuments* ed. Rev. G Townsend 1846 edition.

Introduction

John Hooper was one of the first Protestants to be martyred during the reign of "Bloody Mary" Tudor. An imposing Victorian monument, in the shadow of Gloucester Cathedral, now marks the site of his execution.

He was born around the year 1500 in Somerset, was an only son and had a sister who became a nun. After studying at Oxford he joined the Cistercian order at Cleeve Abbey in north Somerset. On the dissolution of that establishment at the hands of Thomas Cromwell it seems that he gave up his monastic calling in favour of enjoying the pleasures of the Royal court. Yet it was during this time that he first encountered and then embraced the writings and convictions of prominent Continental reformers. The strength of his new faith was such that he had to escape to the Continent to avoid persecution following the introduction of the anti-Protestant "Six Articles" (1539) under Henry VIII. These were transformative years of exile for him. Theologically, he was able to debate first hand with some of the most learned and gifted reformers in Europe.

On a personal level, this period also saw his marriage to Anna de Tserclas and the birth of their first child.

Returning to England following the accession of the zealously Protestant young king Edward VI, Hooper found himself at the heart of the political and religious dramas of the day. Much more is known of these final years of his life thanks to the wealth of writings and correspondence he produced during this period, together with the record found in John Foxe's *Book of Martyrs*. He was chaplain by turns to the two most powerful statesmen in England, the Duke of Somerset and the Earl of Warwick. He was also a close friend of Secretary William Cecil, and a favourite of the King himself. Following his appointment as Bishop of Gloucester, and then also as Bishop of Worcester, he was an active member of the House of Lords and involved in canon law reform. As a writer he was prolific, combative and forensic. Friend and critic alike recognised him as a gifted preacher. As a bishop he was diligent and hard working. He demanded sound faith and high standards of the clergy of the dioceses, and had a deep pastoral concern for the spiritual and physical welfare of his flock.

At times his unwillingness to compromise or adjust his thinking on issues of faith and religion caused frustration and irritation, even in colleagues and allies, and he had a reputation for severity that occasionally preceded him. Yet he was driven by the profound conviction that theology *matters*; that doctrine has consequences for now and for eternity. At the heart of his beliefs was the centrality and all sufficiency of the once for all sacrifice of Jesus Christ as the ground of hope and salvation, and the primacy and truth of the Word of God over human tradition and superstition. It was these two fundamental and incontrovertible principles that led him—one chilly February morning in 1555—to suffer the agonies of a martyr's death.

1

… nay, they looked upon him as some deity

1549

The distance between John Hooper's home county of Somerset, England, and the city-state of Zurich in the Swiss Federation was symbolic of the long spiritual journey he had taken, from Cistercian monk to radical Protestant preacher.

Four years previously, with the Catholicism of Henry VIII making it dangerous for him to remain in England, Hooper had fled to the Continent, and for the last two years had made his home within the Protestant refugee community at Zurich, enjoying the sincere and warm friendship of some of the most influential Protestant theologians of the day—most notably the Swiss-born Heinrich Bullinger, who was Ulrich Zwingli's learned successor as chief pastor of that city. It was an opportunity for him to immerse himself in the reformed doctrines and ideas he had first encountered some years earlier on reading books by Zwingli and Bullinger; doctrines and ideas that had turned his religious world upside down.

Initially Hooper had been content to observe from a distance the religious changes that were beginning to take shape in England under the young King Edward VI. News arrived constantly from correspondents in England and elsewhere in Europe, and he took on the task of translating any letters written in English into the *lingua franca* of Latin. By March 1549, however, the pull of his home country had become irresistible. He realised that it was his duty to return to England to take an active, leading rôle in furthering the cause of religious reform. Yet, for all his deep sense of calling, his departure, when it came towards the end of the month, was still an emotional one. The relationships he had forged in the adversity of exile would remain precious to him for the rest of his life.

It was with mixed feelings that Bullinger addressed the departing Hooper:

> *Master Hooper, although we are sorry to part with your company for our own cause, yet much greater causes we have to rejoice, both for your sake, and especially for the cause of Christ's true religion, that you shall now return, out of long banishment, into your native country again; where not only you may enjoy your own private liberty, but also the cause and state of Christ's church, by you, may fare the better; as we doubt not but it shall … Notwithstanding, with this our*

rejoicing one fear and care we have, lest you, being absent,
and so far distant from us, or else coming to such abundance
of wealth and felicity, in your new welfare and plenty of all
things, and in your flourishing honours, where ye shall come,
peradventure, to be a bishop, and where ye shall find so many
new friends, you will forget us your old acquaintance and well-
willers. Nevertheless, howsoever you shall forget and shake us
off yet this persuade yourself, that we will not forget our old
friend and fellow master Hooper. And if you will please not to
forget us again, then I pray you let us hear from you. [1]

For his part, Hooper warmly thanked all those who had demonstrated such Christian kindness to himself and his family, and promised to keep them informed of all the news in England. But, 'the last news of all I shall not be able to write,'[2] he told his friends. Then, taking Bullinger by the hand, he continued, 'For there where I shall take most pains, there shall you hear of me to be burnt to ashes: and that shall be the last news, which I shall not be able to write unto you; but you shall hear it of me.'

The party that bade farewell to Zurich included Hooper, his wife of two years Anna, their infant daughter Rachel, and Anna's servant Joanna. Soon after their departure—and as if to confirm the rightness of Hooper's decision—Bullinger received a letter from Francis Dryander, a Spanish refugee residing at Cambridge, who expressed an intention to write directly to Hooper, but in the meantime, unaware of recent events, he told Bullinger that he hoped Hooper would:

perform the duty he owes to his country which is sadly

distressed at this time for want of good preachers. And in a calling the most honourable of all others, to lend one's aid to the churches is the duty of a man not only of eminent talent, but of heroic courage; and I think he would do this with dignity.[3]

Events would prove Dryander correct. In the meantime the journey home for Hooper's party was not going to be without danger, since much of Europe was currently under occupation by Imperial troops as part of Emperor Charles V's attempt to create order and stability in his dominions by imposing his pro-Catholic 'Interim'. Travelling by carriage, they arrived at Basle on 27 March 1549. The next day Hooper wrote to Bullinger, in part to apologise to the 'worthy citizen' of Zurich who had generously provided the carriage and horses for this first leg of the long journey home:

That I have been longer delayed upon my journey than he expected, to his inconvenience and my great expense, must be attributed to the roughness of the journey, and not to any loitering on my part or fatigue of the horses. I entreat you to offer my warmest thanks to this excellent man; or else impose this duty of courtesy in my name and at my request upon our very loving friend, master Gaulter, who, if I mistake not, is related either by consanguinity or affinity to the owner of the horses.[4]

Hooper also took the opportunity to send back to Bullinger a sheet, blanket, and pillow he had borrowed, and also a flask which he hoped Bullinger would return to the unknown friend who had supplied it. He left a number of other items at Basle for return at a later date.

From Basle the party travelled on to Strasbourg, arriving on 29 March and expecting to stay for a few days, partly— as he informed Bullinger in a second letter—due to Rachel's teething and Hooper's concern that her 'exposure to the air aggravates the painfulness of incipient illness.'[5] Characteristically, Hooper himself was determined to make the most of any delay in the city. The day after their arrival he attended the morning and evening lectures of Caspar Hedio, Professor of Theology at Strasbourg, and afterwards had dinner with the eminent German reformer Martin Bucer and others.

Sailing from Strasbourg on 2 April, the party stopped at a village near Spires two days later, expecting to have a good meal and take on fresh supplies. Unfortunately, they had been preceded in the village by no less than sixty-four hungry Spanish cavalrymen of the Imperial force, who had all but emptied the hostelries of food and drink, leaving Hooper and his companions with the most meagre of left-overs.

On the fourth day out from Strasbourg the ship ran into terrible river conditions and was thrown about by such high winds and waves that Hooper feared for the safety of everyone on board. Matters were certainly not helped by the 'ignorant and careless sailors,'[6] and Hooper later admitted that, 'unless we had reached the land, which we effected with great difficulty, we should all of us have been lost.' A second ship that had been accompanying them was not so fortunate; not only was its cargo spoiled but the ship's master suffered severe injuries when his leg became entangled in the anchor cable as he attempted to drop anchor. Hooper's party finally landed half a mile from Mayence, and while staying at the *Golden Swan* took the opportunity to exchange news with other travellers.

On 11 April they arrived at Cologne and a week later they had reached the huge, thriving port of Antwerp, where again Hooper had little time for rest. At the request of Sir Philip Hoby, Edward VI's ambassador to the Netherlands, Hooper visited Brussels, which was under occupation by the Emperor's forces. He had hoped to meet with the imprisoned Elector of Saxony, but was prevented from doing so by the Spanish troops guarding him. Returning to Antwerp, Hooper and his party, with their near-shipwreck experience still fresh in their minds, decided to wait to sail with a 'skilful English captain' who was himself waiting for a cargo to take to England. Updating Bullinger on their progress, Hooper added a poignant post-script:

> *After Easter my wife wrote to her mother, who lives about fifteen miles from Antwerp. The messenger found her father dead. Her mother received the letter and gave it my wife's brother to read, who immediately threw it into the fire without reading it. You see the words of Christ are true, that the brother shall persecute the brother for the sake of the word of God.*[7]

As far as her brother was concerned, Anna's acceptance of Protestantism was repugnant; her marriage to a zealous Protestant preacher had put her beyond the pale. Such a scenario was not uncommon amidst the religious revolutions and counter-revolutions of Europe in the middle of the sixteenth century. Hooper's own family back in England was evidence of such religious division.

The final leg of the journey home was completed on 16 May 1549, when Hooper, his family and companions landed on English soil. They immediately travelled on to the sprawling melting pot of London that was to be their home for the next two years—a period of great drama and energetic activity for Hooper.

The England he found on his return was quite different from the England he had left behind. With the death of Henry VIII in January 1547, the political and religious landscape had begun to be transformed, particularly among the ruling élite, if less so among the ordinary people in the country at large. Henry, of course, had had his own personal reasons for removing the Church of England from papal jurisdiction, but his actions had the by-product of smoothing the way for Protestantism. He himself was a Catholic to the end, and his funeral—conducted by the conservative Bishop of Winchester, Stephen Gardiner—was thoroughly Catholic. Yet, with death approaching, Henry had ensured that the Regency Council that would hold the reigns of power with his nine year-old son, Edward, was composed predominantly of Protestant reformers. Edward's uncle, Edward Seymour, now Duke of Somerset, led the Council as first among equals, taking the further title of Lord Protector. Hooper and his family soon took up residence in Somerset's house, and Hooper was appointed his chaplain.

Noticeable by his absence from the list of Council members was Stephen Gardiner. He had been a statesman of prominence and influence during much of Henry's reign;

in particular he had taken a key role in negotiations with the papacy over the annulment of the king's marriage to Katherine of Aragon. He went in and out of royal favour, and more than once survived royal displeasure where others were less fortunate. More importantly in the new religious environment under Edward, he was a staunch Catholic who detested Protestants, once describing them as 'abandoned men, the very dregs of humanity' who 'do not hesitate in the least to despise others in comparison with themselves'.[8] Furthermore, he was against any kind of reform within the Church while the king was so young.[9]

Gardiner and Hooper had crossed paths some years earlier, when Hooper was engaged as steward and chaplain in the house of Sir Thomas Arundel. At that date Hooper was already a convinced Protestant, having devoured some of the writings of Zwingli and Bullinger. His master, Arundel, on the other hand, was a Catholic and sought—as he saw it—to rescue his servant from his heretical Continental doctrines. To that end, he sent Hooper to spend some time with a learned Catholic friend who turned out to be Gardiner, already Bishop of Winchester. After four or five days it was clear that Hooper was not going to alter his opinion, so Gardiner sent him back, commending his learning 'yet bearing in his breast a grudging stomach against master Hooper still.'[10]

The two men later crossed literary swords when on 30 April 1547, soon after he had arrived in Zurich, Hooper received a copy of Gardiner's book entitled *A Detection of the Devil's Sophistrie, wherewith he robbeth the unlearned people, of the true byleef, in the most blessed sacrament of the aulter*, which had been published in

Aldersgate Street, London, in the previous year.[11] Having studied the book, Hooper prepared his response, and in September 1547 published at Zurich *An Answer to my Lord of Wynchesters booke intytlyd a detection of the devyls Sophistrye wherewith he robbith the unlernyd people of the trew byleef in the moost blessyd sacrament of the aulter made by Johann Hoper*. Unfortunately, he had to admit that the book came off the press 'pestered with gross and palpable faults, by passing through the press of an unskilful printer'.[12] Yet while typographical errors clouded some parts, they could not obscure Hooper's fundamental case or weaken the passion of his arguments. He meticulously, forcefully, and at times almost mockingly, pummelled away at Gardiner's 'obstinate' and 'blind' position. As always his arguments were grounded in Scripture and drew from the Church Fathers and other eminent theologians from across the centuries. Step by step he refuted the real presence of Christ in the bread, declaring that a 'bastard is this transubstantiation doubtless'.[13] He moved on to assert that no sacrament had any power in itself if it was not received with faith, and he also found space to attack the timeserving bishops who neglected their flocks.

Hooper and Gardiner would continue to fight over this same ground in the following years, eventually confronting each other face to face. For now, Gardiner found himself swimming against the powerful tide of religious change while Hooper was setting the agenda for reform.

Once in London Hooper wasted no time in setting to work. Preaching with great energy and regularity—at least once a day, and mostly twice—he drew huge crowds of people and the churches were often packed to the doors.

His delivery and voice were later likened to 'the most melodious sound and tune of Orpheus's harp'.[14] Yet his sermons were never designed to soothe or entertain his hearers; rather, he spoke passionately and eloquently to correct sin, attack the wickedness of the world, and highlight the corruption that ran throughout the church. Again, what drove him was his unshakeable belief in the truth of the Bible, the word of God. Such was the effect he had on those who thronged to hear him that the Oxford academic, Dr Richard Smith, who was a particular critic of Hooper and other Protestants, declared sarcastically that Hooper was 'so admired by the people, that they held him for a prophet; nay, they looked upon him as some deity.'[15] Those were not the only feathers to be ruffled. Hooper was attacked and libelled, and sometimes his opponents deposited their libels into his pulpit even as he preached. One zealous Protestant, Edward Underhill, took on the task of refuting those libels on Hooper's behalf; on occasions he nailed his written answers Luther-like to the doors of certain London churches. For his rôle in defending the increasingly renowned preacher, Underhill became known as 'Hooper's champion'; at one point he even intervened to prevent the possible imprisonment of John Day, one of Hooper's printers.[16]

Although preaching was his clear priority, Hooper hoped also to find time to journey to his home county of Somerset to visit his parents. The last time he had seen them was when he returned briefly from the Continent to ask for financial help ahead of his marriage to Anna. His relationship with his Catholic father in particular was not an easy one. He once confessed to Bullinger: 'My

father, of whom I am the only son and heir, is so opposed
to me on account of Christ's religion, that should I refuse
to act according to his wishes, I shall be sure to find him
for the future, not a father, but a cruel tyrant'.[17] Despite
the tensions, he still intended to see his parents at the
earliest opportunity. Unfortunately the West Country
was not the best place to visit during the summer of 1549.
Widespread unrest had been stirred by accumulating
economic and social problems combined with popular
reaction against the imposition of Protestant reforms in the
shape of the new Prayer Book and the Act of Uniformity.
Rebellion and disorder was growing. As the rebels became
more organised, their leaders—who were mostly Catholic
clergy—drew up a set of demands to present to the
Council. In content these were in effect calling for a return
to the Catholicism of Henry's reign; in tone they were
strident and lacked deferent respect. Attempts to quell
the rebellions were slow, and hampered by the fact that
local Catholic gentry, while not throwing their weight
behind the rebels, were very unwilling to act against the
rebels on behalf of the Council. Finally, new troops were
sent under Provost Marshall Sir Anthony Kingston, a
knight of Gloucestershire, who had been instrumental in
crushing the 'Pilgrimage of Grace' uprising during the reign
of Henry VIII. He ruthlessly brought the West Country
rebellion to a bloody end by the middle of August, gaining
in the process a lasting reputation for cold brutality,
notably at Bodmin, where he enjoyed the hospitality of the
mayor and then proceeded to have him hanged as a traitor.

As it turned out, even with order being restored to the

West Country there were soon fresh matters to occupy Hooper's mind, time and energy.

2

... vile heretics and beasts[18]

On 1 September 1549 the conservative Bishop of London, Edmund Bonner, came to preach at St Paul's. He had been Gardiner's chaplain and shared the Bishop of Winchester's antipathy towards the ongoing Protestant reforms. The Council had ordered him to use the sermon to condemn the recent rebellions over the Prayer Book, to assert that external ceremonies were of no value without true faith, and in particular, to make it clear to his hearers that the young king Edward possessed complete royal authority in spite of his age.

Bonner was already sailing close to the wind. Early in Edward's reign he had spent a brief period confined in the Fleet prison for refusing to implement Protestant reforms within his diocese. Now, in direct defiance of the Council, he not only failed to comply with the order but compounded his disobedience by preaching in defence of the Catholic doctrine of transubstantiation—Hooper and Gardiner's chief battleground. That same day Hooper himself took up the gauntlet and preached against Bonner. Later, supported by another Protestant preacher, William Latimer—who had formerly been one of Anne Boleyn's chaplains—Hooper wrote a bill of complaint to the king regarding the Bishop of London's defiance. As the two men had been eyewitnesses to Bonner's sermon their joint statement was able to confirm what had, and had not, been said. They assured the king that in bringing the matter to his attention they were 'not moved of any malice, grudge, envy, or evil will to the person of the bishop, but constrained by the love and zeal which we bear towards your highness, and of our duty and allegiance to your majesty'. They concluded by humbly asking that Bonner should be called to account and that further action should be taken against him.

On 8 September the king and Council appointed a small commission headed by Archbishop Cranmer and including Nicholas Ridley, Bishop of Rochester, to deal with the issue. Two days later Bonner was called to appear before the commission at Lambeth palace. From the outset he demonstrated complete contempt for the proceedings by refusing to remove his cap when he entered the room where the commission was assembled, and by ignoring the eminent men sitting in judgement over him. When he did finally speak he was rude and sarcastic. Martin Micron, one of Hooper's friends who was present at this hearing, later told Bullinger that Bonner 'behaved with so much effrontery and stubbornness … that you would rather call him a buffoon than a bishop.'[19]

Formal proceedings against Bonner began with the reading of the king's letter confirming the purpose and authority of the commission. When Hooper and Latimer were called forward to give their evidence, Bonner's response was to mock his accusers, saying of them that 'one speaks like a goose, the other like a woodcock'.

Personal abuse was not the only tactic Bonner employed in his defence. He declared the allegations against him to be too general to be answered specifically, and then, in order to divert the focus away from the subject of his wilful disobedience, he suddenly began addressing the question of the real presence in the sacrament of the Lord's supper, trying to create the impression that he was principally being attacked on a matter of doctrine rather than discipline. He deliberately attempted to disrupt and sidetrack proceedings by urging Cranmer to enter into debate on the matter there and then. Cranmer, however, wisely refused to take the bait and drew the meeting to a close by giving Bonner a few days in which to prepare an answer to the charges laid against him.

Bonner was back before the commission on 13 September and immediately sought to disrupt proceedings on the grounds of a legal technicality, pointing out that one of the commissioners present, Sir Thomas Smith—one of the king's Principal Secretaries—had not been present at the first hearing and therefore was ineligible to sit at this second one. Members of the commission could not hide their frustration. Cranmer stated that 'if the law be so indeed, surely I take it to be an unreasonable law'. The king's other Principal Secretary, Sir William Petre, confessed himself rusty in legal minutiae but told Bonner, 'for you to stick in such trifling matters, you shall rather in my judgement hurt yourself and your matter, than otherwise'. Sir Thomas Smith himself, no doubt resenting being the centre of contention, declared Bonner's tactics to be 'but quidities and quirks invented to delay matters'.

Bonner had clearly wrong-footed his opponents and had certainly succeeded in creating a degree of confusion, but he realised that any delay would only be temporary and therefore did not press the point further. Instead he took out his statement and contrived to be permitted to read it out rather than merely submit it, by suggesting that the haste in which it had been written had rendered it illegible to anyone but himself. His main line of defence took the form of a long, highly personal attack on his 'pretensed denunciators', Hooper and Latimer, in a clear attempt to undermine their credibility as witnesses. He labelled them 'infamed, notorious criminous persons, and also open and manifest heretics'. Hooper's preaching, he said, was full of 'poisoned and venomous doctrine' and 'erroneous, detestable, and abominable errors' that were 'infecting and poisoning the king's subjects'. Such men deserved to be 'excluded, avoided, detested, eschewed, and abhorred, in all manner of wise, of all faithful and true christian people, fearing God, and desiring the advancement of the truth'. Bonner was particularly indignant that he, the Bishop of London, had been so blatantly attacked from the most important pulpit in his very own diocese.

At the next session on Monday 16 September Hooper and Latimer were given the right to reply. Hooper—who was at that time still residing in the home of the Duke of Somerset—refuted Bonner's accusation that he, Hooper, was a heretic and kept the company of heretics, and made it clear that by inference Bonner was accusing the Lord Protector of being a heretic, of aiding and abetting a heretic, and of actively encouraging and enjoying heretical preaching.

There followed a fierce confrontation. Bonner, resorting once more to personal abuse, called Hooper a 'varlet'—a scoundrel—and then tried to read something supposedly incriminating from one of Hooper's published books. When Hooper interrupted him, Bonner shouted impatiently, 'Put your pipes; you have spoken for your part; I will meddle no more with you', and carried on reading. His whole manner was met with laughter from the members of the public present, which only riled him more, until he turned on them too, calling them 'woodcocks'. Cranmer too found himself on the receiving end of Bonner's ranting. Finally, Bonner provided the hearing with twenty questions to be put to Hooper and Latimer, again challenging their character, doctrine, and reliability as witnesses.

The king, having been informed that Bonner was still complaining about the validity of the proceedings, and aware too of Bonner's continual prevarication, next day wrote a letter to make it absolutely clear that the members of the commission had full authority to deal with the matter as they saw fit and should proceed by 'cutting away all vain and superfluous delays, and having respect to the only truth of the matter'. Even this made no difference to Bonner's attitude. When he next appeared before the commission, on 18 September, in the great hall at Lambeth, he declared that he came 'under protestation of the nullity and invalidity, injustice and iniquity, of your pretensed and unlawful process made by you against me.'

The following day he failed to appear at all, apparently due to illness. By Friday 20 September he was clearly a desperate man, becoming increasingly angry and volatile. He again attacked Sir Thomas Smith—this time accusing him of being motivated by personal malice—and was still frustrated that Hooper and other 'vile heretics and beasts' should be given licence to preach at Paul's Cross 'and so infect and betray my flock'.

As he was unceremoniously taken off to be held in the Marshalsea prison he angrily rounded on Cranmer: 'Well, my lord!' he shouted, 'I am sorry that I, being a bishop, am thus handled at your grace's hand; but more sorry that ye suffer abominable heretics to practice as they do in London and elsewhere, infecting and disquieting the king's liege people!'

The following Monday he was declared 'contumax'—obstinate—and found guilty of the charges against him. On 1 October he was finally deprived of the bishopric of London and returned to the Marshalsea.

'Should he be again restored to his office and Episcopal function', Hooper later told Bullinger while relating news of his bitter personal confrontation with Bonner, 'I shall, I doubt not, be restored to my country and my Father which is in heaven.'[20]

There was, however, yet another significant drama unfolding during the summer of 1549.

3

… or else we must perish

The position of Hooper's patron, the Duke of Somerset, was becoming precarious. Politically, he was continuing to pursue a war with Scotland despite the spiralling and crippling costs, and in the country there was widespread discontent over the religious reforms and social and economic changes. Other members of the Regency Council had become increasingly irritated by his tight, isolationist grip on the reigns of power and were suspicious of his tactics. Somerset certainly did not help himself by his inherent lack of wisdom and tact. His perceived weakness in dealing with the West Country rebellion and Kett's rebellion in East Anglia over the summer was the final straw. By the end of the summer, secret meetings were taking place in London and plots were being hatched. Catching wind of what was happening, on 6 October 1549 he fled with the king and a number of supporters to the relative security of Windsor Castle. His only hope was to encourage others to rally to his side by claiming that the king himself was in danger. This last throw of the dice failed. By 11 October, recognising the hopelessness of his situation, he agreed to surrender to the Council. On 14 October he was sent to the Tower, while those who had supported him at Windsor were placed under house arrest. Hooper, writing to Bullinger at the beginning of November, expressed a good deal of apprehension about Somerset's fate. Not surprisingly, he also informed his friend in Zurich: 'I have been so overwhelmed by difficult and constant business since my arrival in England, that I have not yet been able to visit my native place or my parents.'[21]

One piece of 'difficult and constant business' had arisen as the result of his views on divorce as expressed in his recently published *A Declaration of the ten holy commandmentes of allmygthye God.*[22] In the chapter concerning the seventh commandment—*Thou shalt commit none adultery*—he had maintained that, according to God's word, divorce was only permitted on the grounds of adultery, or in the case of 'infidelity', by which he meant that one of the married couple was an 'infidel', ie. not a Christian. Crucially, however, he went on to declare the equal rights of the sexes in such instances. These 'few words', as Hooper later described them, had drawn him into an ongoing controversy in which, amongst other things, he was accused of undermining the dignity and sanctity of marriage.

Meanwhile, pressing affairs of state were occupying his thoughts. By the end of December he recognised that the fate of England and the progress of reform hung in the balance. It was a time of great uncertainty and danger, but he remained hopeful: 'Although our vessel is dangerously tossed about on all sides,' he said, 'yet God in his providence holds the helm, and raises up more favourers of his word in his majesty's councils, who with activity and courage defend the cause of Christ.'[23] For the time being at least his hope was not in vain. The Protestant cause still had Archbishop Cranmer, who retained much influence with the king; two new appointments to the Council had strengthened the reforming party, while the remaining conservative members were removed. Most importantly, the man who emerged as the new *de facto* leader of the Council, John Dudley, Earl of Warwick, continued the process of reform begun under Somerset. Warwick was wise enough not to assume the politically loaded title of Lord Protector, but instead became Lord President of the Council, signalling a new, more conciliar approach to government.

Significantly, Hooper's own position did not suffer as a result of Somerset's fall from power. It was not long before he was appointed chaplain to Warwick, and in a letter to Bullinger written just after Christmas he spoke of his increasingly cordial relations with Archbishop Cranmer.[24] Moreover, he was highly respected and favoured by the young king. In turn, he was so impressed by Edward's learning and, no doubt, his increasingly zealous Protestantism, that he declared the king to be 'such an one for his age as the world has never seen.'[25] He enthused to Bullinger, 'you have never seen in the world for these thousand years so much erudition united with piety and sweetness of disposition. Should he live and grow up with these virtues he will be a terror to all the sovereigns of the earth.'[26]

Hooper's access to court, where he had become a regular preacher, also enabled him to observe the progress of Edward's half-sister, Elizabeth, with whom he was equally impressed:

> His sister, the daughter of the late king by queen Ann [Boleyn], is inflamed with the same zeal for the religion of Christ. She not only knows what the true religion is, but has acquired such proficiency in Greek and Latin, that she is able to defend it by the most just arguments and the most happy talent; so that she encounters few adversaries whom she does not overcome.[27]

Elizabeth's reign as queen would prove Hooper a most perceptive judge.

With the natural pride of a father, Hooper was also thrilled with the progress of his precocious daughter Rachel, who was not quite two years old. Bullinger had baptised Rachel and was one of her godparents, so he took a keen interest in her welfare and education. Hooper gladly reported to him that she was already learning well and could understand English, German and French, and had a particular flair for Latin.[28]

As if to underline the esteem in which he was still held despite the events of the previous months, on 5 February 1550 Hooper was appointed to preach before the king and Council on every Wednesday during Lent. It was an

important opportunity, and one to be grasped with both
hands.

Taking as his text the Old Testament book of Jonah,
he expounded the meaning of each section and boldly
applied it to his eminent audience, and to the current
condition of England as he saw it. His approach, which
had been developed and honed by regular and constant
preaching, was methodical and meticulous; combining
a profound, lively knowledge of Scripture with a sincere
and passionate desire to warn, instruct, and exhort. In his
epistle introducing the series he encapsulated his basic
theme:

> *Among all other most noble and famous deeds of kings and
> princes, none is more godly, commendable, nor profitable to
> the commonwealth, than to promote and set forth unto their
> subjects the pure and sincere religion of the eternal God, King
> of all kings, and Lord of all lords. Then shall justice, peace, and
> concord reign, the door of idolatry be shut up, by the which
> entered all evil, and kings and kingdoms fallen into jeopardy,
> as the writings of the prophets do testify.*

At the very end of the series, he concluded, sounding
much like an Old Testament prophet himself:

> *If your majesty do these things, the blood of your people
> shall not be required at your hands. But I rede both king and
> council to be admonished, and to amend things amiss: if
> not, the king of Ninive [Nineveh] with his people shall rise at
> the latter day, and condemn both king and council to death:
> for they converted at the preaching of one man, yea, at the*

*preaching of a stranger; we have not only heard the same by
the mouth of strangers, but also by the mouth of our own
countrymen, and that many times. Let us therefore believe
and amend, or else we must perish.*[29]

This call to believe and amend was a call for the king and
Council to obey God by rejecting idolatry, superstition, and
the inventions of men, and by pursuing social justice. In
practical terms that principally—though not exclusively—
meant ridding the land of the last vestiges of Catholicism
on the one hand, and putting in its place the 'true'
religion of Protestantism on the other, and specifically the
Protestantism of Zurich. As Hooper explained from the
start, such 'true' religion and the doctrine upon which it
stood was no novelty, but was as old as the religion of the
apostles and prophets. This was in contrast to what he
called the 'new' religion of the 'papists'. In these sermons
he fiercely attacked the whole institutional machinery,
doctrine, and practice of the Roman Catholic Church. He
described the seat of Rome as 'the nest of abomination', a
place which clearly did not reflect the spirit of service and
sacrifice of Christ and Peter, but rather 'the patrimony
of Judas and Simon Magus… more ease than pain, more
riches than burden'. Bishops and priests, he declared, were
'like thieves and murderers' who do 'the abomination
commanded by man, with massing, conjuring the holy-
water bucket, and such like'. The king and council should be
commended for the reforms already made, he said, without
which the people of England would still be oppressed
by 'the violent and cruel tyranny of antichrist'. Patron
saints were denounced and the pope himself—the office,

not the individual—was declared as one that 'sleepeth and delighteth in his sin'. Church altars should rightly be replaced by tables, he said, 'for as long as the altars remain, both the ignorant people, and the ignorant evil-persuaded priest, will dream always of sacrifice', and Christ's once-offered sacrifice could never by repeated. For Hooper, the written word of God was 'as perfect as God himself' and 'needeth not that blasphemous and stinking help of the bishop of Rome'.

In the fifth and sixth sermons he dealt at length with that perennially thorny and divisive issue of the Lord's Supper, in particular the meaning and significance of Christ's words of institution, 'This is my body'. During the reign of Henry VIII many Protestants, including Hooper, had fled abroad in the wake of the Six Articles of 1539. In addition to forbidding priests to marry, these Articles particularly offended Protestants with their affirmation of the Catholic doctrine of transubstantiation.

To Hooper, such doctrine was anathema. Following the teaching of Zwingli, he now declared to king and Council that, 'The sacraments be as visible words offered unto the eyes and other senses, as the sweet sound of the word to the ear, and the Holy Ghost to the heart'. Therefore, he continued, 'the bread in the holy supper [is] called the body of Christ, and the wine the blood of Christ, because they be sacraments and seals of God's promises in Christ'. In a dense and detailed section he systematically propounded this view, citing evidence from Scripture, the Church Fathers, and even papal canon law. Not only was the Catholic position torn down, but so too was the convoluted Lutheran middle-way that had Christ really present in, with, and under the bread since Jesus' glorified flesh was held to be capable of multi-presence. Hooper had not changed his view of Luther's doctrine of the Lord's Supper since he had told Bullinger back in 1546 that Luther's position made him 'more erroneous [in that particular] than all the papists'.

Concerning baptism too he was equally forthright, again attacking superstition. Alluding once more to the nautical backdrop to his text he colourfully prescribed what should be done to such superstitious practices: 'I pray the king's majesty and his most honourable council to prepare a ship, as soon as may be, to send them home again to their mother church, the bosom and breast of man'.

His attacks upon Roman Catholicism were not, however, primarily motivated by sheer blind prejudice, although there was certainly an element of that. His motivation, as always, was his unswerving belief in the truth and sufficiency of Scripture and in the ideal of the New Testament church. When, in a letter to Bullinger written soon after his arrival back home, he had declared mournfully, 'How dangerously our England is afflicted by heresies of this land, God only knows,' he was not speaking of Catholicism but of anabaptist sects. He chose his targets, not according to their association with the bishop of Rome but according to their diversion from the word of God.

The Lenten sermons also revealed a side to Hooper's character that would emerge more fully during his time at Gloucester. For him theology had practical consequences for individuals and society, and for social justice in particular. In uncompromising terms he condemned the 'ravening and covetous noblemen that with injuries and

wrongs now afflict the poor' and who 'in vain glory and
pride of the mammon of the world... condemn and disdain
the very image of God in the poor'. In the same way, he
attacked dishonest and deceitful lawyers who received
'rewards and bribes, which blindeth the eyes', describing
their activities as 'a noble kind of thievery'. Quoting from
the book of Proverbs, he reminded his hearers that, 'He
that quitteth the evil doer, and condemneth the innocent,
be both execrable and damned before God'. All men should
beware of how they gain material wealth, how they keep
it, and how they use it. Those who wickedly acquire such
wealth by means of 'murder, rape, violency, craft or theft,
subtleties, frauds, corruption of laws, by lying, flattery,
and such other' must make restitution, as Zacchaeus the
tax collector did (Luke 19). In their comfort, those who
hold such wealth must also beware the dangers of pride,
forgetting God, and taking life too easily. Finally, in the use
of wealth, they should avoid excess and dissipation, and
not neglect the poor and needy, as the rich man ignored
Lazarus the beggar at his gate (Luke 16).

On the other hand, while Hooper deplored the abuse of
civil and ecclesiastical power and the injustice done to the
poor, he still believed that evil and wrongdoing must not
be ignored but, for the sake of the whole realm and all its
people, must be strictly and firmly addressed:

> Among the citizens be a great number that trouble the
> ship also, as adulterous unpunished, the fraud and guile of
> the merchandise, idleness the mother of all mischief, theft,
> murder, blasphemous oaths, conspiracy and treason, with
> open slander and rebuke of God's most holy word. These

*things and such like tosseth the poor ship, that hardly she can
sail above the water; and so displeaseth the majesty of God,
that he will never cease from sending of tempests, till those
Jonases [Jonahs] be amended or cast into the sea.*

The sermons may have been uncompromising and
forthright, but for the main part they were not particularly
controversial. There was one exception to this, however,
which proved to be particularly important as a sign of
things to come.

In his third sermon, preached on 3 March 1550, he briefly
but pointedly criticised the recently instituted Ordinal for
the ordination of deacons and priests, and the consecration
of bishops. His criticisms centred on three issues.

First, he objected to the requirement for candidates to
swear by saints. In his *Declaration of Christe and of his
offyce*, written while in exile, first printed in Zurich in 1547,
he had already made his view crystal clear:

*What intolerable ill, blasphemy of God, and ethnical
[heathenish] idolatry is this, to admit and teach the invocation
of saints departed out of this world! It taketh from God his
true honour; it maketh him a fool, that only hath ordained
only Christ to be Mediator between man and him. It
diminisheth the merits of Christ, taketh from the law of God
her perfection and majesty, whereas [wherein] God hath
opened his will and pleasure unto the world in all things. It
condemneth the old church of the patriarchs and prophets,
likewise the church of the apostles and martyrs, that never
taught the invocation of saints.*[30]

At the conclusion of the first Lenten sermon he had exhorted his hearers to 'forsake that heretical doctrine that divideth your hearts in prayer, part to God, and part to saints departed; for God is sufficient to help, and will help alone'. Now he went further. Although his actual reference to the Ordinal oath with its swearing by saints was little more than passing, its importance was trailed by a detailed and—by his own admission—long preamble in which he provided example after example from Scripture to demonstrate the power and truth of his position. He continued this point by again urging his hearers to take action and to 'beseech God to restore us to the primitive church, which never yet had nor shall have any match or like', concluding, as if to stress the importance of the matter, 'Before all things beware of an oath by any creatures, except ye will be glad to have God's displeasure'.

Hooper's second concern regarding the Ordinal was the requirement for candidates to wear white vestments. He was adamant that such a requirement could not be found in the word of God 'nor yet in the primitive and best church'. Moreover, to his mind, it was 'rather the habit and vesture of Aaron and the gentiles, than of the ministers of Christ'. His attack lasted no more than three sentences on this occasion, but he returned to the subject again later. In the seventh sermon he stated that the use of such vestments and priestly apparel obscured the ministry of Christ's church. Furthermore—and critically for Hooper— ministers 'should not be known by their vestments and shavings [the tonsure], but by their doctrine'. For now he had made his point, but within a matter of weeks the issue was to take on a far deeper significance.

His third concern over the Ordinal led him to question certain aspects of the ceremonials, in particular, 'where, and of whom, and when have they learned, that he that is called to the ministry of God's word, should hold the bread and chalice in one hand and the book in the other hand?'. He knew of course that such a practice could not be found in Scripture or in the primitive church. 'Why', he continued ironically, 'do they not as well give him in his hand the fount and the water [for baptism]? For the one is a sacrament as well as the other. If the fount is too great, take him a basin with water, or such like vessel?'

Within days of delivering his third sermon, Hooper was summoned to appear before Archbishop Cranmer and the Council to explain his attack upon the Ordinal. The meeting turned out to be long and heated, with Cranmer taking the lead and speaking particularly forthrightly. He no doubt saw Hooper's words as being as much a challenge to his own authority, and the authority of the Church, as of oaths, vestments, and ceremonial. The meeting demonstrated the fact that even among those who were supporters of and activists for reform, there were real differences regarding the extent and pace of change. As his sermons demonstrated, Hooper was certainly on the wing of those who desired—even demanded—wholesale reform to bring about a church in England that was more in line with the doctrine, practice, and appearance of the reformed Continental churches, particularly those in Zurich which, according to him were themselves more in line with the ideal of the primitive church. For the time being, however, a compromise was agreed, by which Hooper himself was not required to wear vestments, except when preaching at court, but those who wanted to wear them would not be prevented from doing so. When he related the events to Bullinger, Hooper admitted the difficulties but concluded that 'at length the end and issue was for the glory of God'.[31] In the same letter, written on 27 March, 1550, the day after he completed the Lenten series, he made it perfectly clear, however, that his opinion of the Ordinal had not changed. 'I am so much offended with that book', he wrote, 'and that not without abundant reason, that if it not be corrected, I neither can nor will communicate with the church in the administration of the [Lord's] supper'.[32]

As if all this was not enough, during this period Hooper also had a fresh controversy from a more expected quarter and with an old adversary. Stephen Gardiner, who was by now imprisoned in the Tower without charge, challenged him to a public debate over his views on the Lord's Supper. Recent events had proved that Hooper was never one to avoid a confrontation, and he expressed his willingness to accept such a challenge. At this point Gardiner may have got cold feet because he made a pre-condition that he must have known would not be met; he wanted to be released from his incarceration to attend the debate. His demand was duly rejected and what would have been a remarkable set-piece confrontation had to wait for another time. Instead, Gardiner spent the next months putting his views to paper in a work entitled *A discussion of Mr Hoper's oversight where he entreateth amonge his other Sermons the matter of the Sacrament of the Bodye and Blood of Christe.*[33]

Despite the controversies with the Council, Hooper had again lost no favour. At Easter, the king and Council informed him that they were to grant him the bishopric of Gloucester, which had remained vacant since the first incumbent, John Wakeman, had died in the previous year.

4

… this turbulent tempest[34]

The grant of a bishopric was the sort of gift that most clerics would have eagerly and gratefully received. Hooper, however, refused to accept it; a decision he could not have taken lightly. First of all, such appointments were *granted* not *offered*, and appointees were expected to accept without question. Second, to reject the appointment was to say 'no' to the king and Council—God's appointed authorities on earth. Third, the grounds for Hooper's rejection of the bishopric were technically a breach of civil law under the Act of Uniformity of the previous year, and he therefore risked incurring imprisonment and the forfeiture of one year's income for a first offence. A short while later he explained to Bullinger that he had taken the decision 'both by reason of the shameful and impious form of the oath, which all who choose to undertake the function of a bishop are compelled to put up with, and also on account of those Aaronic habits which they still retain in that calling, and are used to wear, not only at the administration of the sacraments, but also at public prayers'.

Not surprisingly, Hooper was immediately summoned to appear before the king to explain himself, but Edward accepted that his reservations were in fact valid. On 15 March 1550 he was summoned before the Council, and although the discussions were again heated, he won the day with support from the recently released and reinstated Duke of Somerset. As he wrote triumphantly to Bullinger, he was appointed free from 'all defilement of superstition and from the imposition of the oath'. On 3 July Letters Patent were issued, formally confirming the grant of the bishopric of Gloucester to Hooper. Unfortunately this was far from the end of the matter, and the Protestant martyrologist John Foxe had to admit later that through the subsequent unseemly contention 'occasion was given to true Christians to lament, and to their adversaries to rejoice'.[35]

All seemed straight forward enough. On 20 July Hooper was again before the king and Council to discuss the matter of the oath, and once more he convinced the king of the strength of his argument. In a moment of high drama that must have gladdened Hooper the king declared, 'What wickedness is here, Hooper? Are these offices ordained in the name of saints or of God?', and, in front of everybody personally crossed out the offending part of the oath. Three days later, the Earl of Warwick sent a letter to Archbishop Cranmer confirming Hooper's right to be excused the reference to saints in the oath of consecration.

In turn, Cranmer referred Hooper on to Nicholas Ridley, now Bishop of London in place of Bonner, who was due to perform the consecration. Here was where the real problems began. The issue now turned from the oath to vestments.

Ridley had a BA and MA from Cambridge, and had spent a period in Paris and Louvain, before becoming one of Cranmer's chaplains. Although he had embraced a number of reformed doctrines during the precarious later years of the reign of Henry VIII, he had maintained a low enough profile not to feel the need to flee abroad as Hooper had done. He had been granted the bishopric of Rochester in 1547 and was promoted to the see of London in April 1550 following the deprivation of Bonner. He was a leading reformer and no traditionalist, having already ordered the removal of altars throughout his diocese, for example. On his appointment Hooper had described him as a 'pious and learned man', but added, 'if only his new dignity do not change his conduct'.[36]

However, Ridley refused to consecrate Hooper using any form of service other than that which had been legally prescribed by parliament. Here the issue was not only a question of words and vestments but of authority. It seems he had been willing to bend the rules in the consecration of Robert Farrar as Bishop of St David's, and in the ordination of deacons John Bradford and Thomas Sampson, but Ridley clearly viewed Hooper's stand as an arrogant and dangerous challenge to the church's authority, not to mention parliament's authority. The highly respected Italian reformer Peter Martyr, who had a teaching position at Oxford, made this point in a letter to Bullinger some months later:

> as nearly two years have elapsed since the mass was abrogated by the general parliament (as they call it) of this realm, and a certain administration of the Lord's supper appointed, in which some vestments are assigned to the ministers of the church; it is very offensive to the king's councillors, and to very many others, both among the nobility and commonalty, that a decree publicly received, and confirmed by the authority of the kingdom, should be found fault with as ungodly, and condemned as though it were at variance with the sacred writings.[37]

Ridley also had a genuine and understandable fear of disorder if individuals were permitted unbridled freedom in matters of doctrine and church practice. He may well have been resentful of Hooper's rôle in the establishment in London of a 'Strangers Church' of refugee Protestants from a number of Continental areas, under the leadership of an old friend of Hooper's from the Zurich days, the Polish-born John à Lasco. By royal decree no less, the Bishop of London had no jurisdiction over this church. Ridley understandably viewed the presence of an un-regulated radical congregation in his own diocese as a dangerous development.[38]

In the middle of all this another imprint of what Hooper described as his 'little declaration upon the Ten Commandments' was published by Richard Jugge in London. Hooper found it necessary to include a new preface to this edition in which he strenuously defended his controversial views on divorce against the 'foolish judgement of foolishly and ignorant people, that now speaketh slanderously of one unslanderous doctrine'.[39] Characteristically, he was angry that his words and intention had been misunderstood.

In this new edition he also added a number of pages to the chapter on the seventh commandment in which he clarified and defended his doctrine of divorce and stated again the equality of the sexes in the matter. It was clear to him that many of those who opposed his views had not even read his book. Furthermore, they had not raised their concerns with him personally. Consequently, he challenged them to read his book and then be prepared to debate any subsequent disagreements at a public disputation before judges of their choosing, or through private correspondence. He simply desired to be judged according to the word of God, and to receive a fair, impartial hearing: 'Wherefore, my friend, of friendship be not too friendly to favour me too much;' he wrote, 'nor thou, mine enemy, of enmity condemn me not too soon'.

In order to directly refute accusations that his views somehow trivialised marriage, he inserted a number of very practical steps a couple should take to avoid divorce, including arbitration.

Meanwhile, the controversy over vestments showed no signs of abating. On 30 July Hooper returned to the Council to restate his position. Ridley then secretly approached the Council and succeeded in turning many members against Hooper and in favour of his own position. Such tactics merely served to harden Hooper's already intransigent attitude. Over the next couple of months

Hooper put together a written statement of his position and submitted it to the Council on 3 October. Ridley in turn delivered his own written case to the Council. Both men took the Bible very seriously indeed, but the issue of vestments demonstrated their differing views in terms of how the Bible should be used in determining church practice.

In his submission Hooper developed what he had touched on in the Lenten sermons, stating that since Scripture did not expressly *command* or *support* the use of vestments by church ministers, such vestments should not be used. Ridley, on the other hand, believed that since Scripture did not expressly *forbid* their use, vestments were not intrinsically wrong but rather were 'things indifferent' which should be used according to the authority of the Church. Hooper believed that, following the Protestant doctrine of the priesthood of all believers, there should be no external distinctions among Christians; none should be set apart from the rest on account of their dress. He also felt that the use of vestments was a dangerous vestige of Roman Catholicism, and went as far as suggesting that those who persisted with such vestments were 'papists'. This was as unfair as it was untrue, and the sort of uncharitable remark that no doubt prompted Foxe's sadness. Ridley was no more temperate, casting at Hooper the other great slur that could be laid at a Protestant, that he was an 'anabaptist'. Given that under Edward it was two extreme Protestants (albeit Unitarians), Joan Bocher and George van Parris who were the only so called heretics to be burned at the stake, Ridley's accusation could easily have had serious repercussions. In later years, and under very different circumstances, Ridley was to express his own sadness at the way in which the whole affair was conducted.[40]

Debate spread beyond the two protagonists and the Council. The views of prominent and influential Continental reformers now living in England were sought and offered. One of these was John à Lasco who had gained some knowledge of the intrigues of the English church during the previous winter months, having stayed at Lambeth Palace with Cranmer. After a brief return to the Continent earlier in the year, he was back in London in May to lead the 'Strangers Church', and so it was not surprising that he emphatically took Hooper's side.

He not only shared Hooper's theology but also was of a similar bold temperament. He entered the controversy by writing a colourful, allegorical letter to the king in which he avoided any direct reference to the protagonists or the central issue of vestments but succeeded in making his own position crystal clear. Edward, he declared, was a father whose daughter—the English Church—had been rescued from the Romish brothel:

> But the same father, if he be wise, thinketh it not enough for the safety of his daughter, and the honour of his house, that he hath brought her home again, unless he take from her wholly whatsoever he knoweth to be accounted in those houses an whorish attire: neither doth he inquire whence such attire came first, but judgeth it dishonourable to himself, and so unworthy his daughter, and whole family, that any such thing at all, as strumpets have used for dressing in their houses, should appear in his.[41]

Moreover, he continued, such a father must also maintain the family reputation among his neighbours and the city as a whole. It was a delusion to think that what was done *inside* the house did not have an effect *outside* it. In other words, the young king's high calling brought with it a responsibility towards Christians within England and elsewhere to 'remove from the ministry of the sacraments all these Popish trinkets, wherewith it hath been fearfully profaned, and restore unto it again the virgin-like attire, wherewith it was of old adorned'. In so doing, his esteem and reputation within the Christian world would grow even more.

Hooper, writing to Bullinger in December, was to say that, 'Master à Lasco alone of all the foreigners who have any influence, stood on my side.'[42] This comment probably reflected the increasing sense of isolation that Hooper felt, but also expressed a sense of genuine gratitude towards à Lasco, and some disappointment at the lack of support from other reformers.

The two most influential reforming 'foreigners' living in England at that time were Peter Martyr and the German-born Martin Bucer. If Hooper felt let down by their response to the controversy, his sentiments were quite understandable but not wholly fair. In fact, Martyr and Bucer were broadly in agreement with his views on vestments, but they were in nature far more conciliatory, patient, and—in this sensitive matter at least—wise. Martyr, writing to Bullinger, expressed his feeling that, 'All things cannot be done in a moment, and there must be labour and time for this misshapen embryo to attain its proper symmetry and shape.'[43] Along with Hooper, the two men would have liked to have seen vestments done away with and more reform undertaken, but they were far more concerned about the damaging effects of the dispute and the need to address more pressing matters such as the lack of good preachers to minister the word of God to the people. In November, Bucer candidly told Hooper, 'This controversy afflicts me exceedingly, since it places such an impediment in the way of yourself and others. What would I not have given to prevent its outbreak, or to repress and extinguish it instantly.'[44]

The matter dragged on and much of the year was taken up with its controversy. In the midst of it all, or perhaps to step out from it for a while, Hooper finally managed to visit his parents for a fortnight at Whitsun and was pleased to find that his father, 'though not a friend to the gospel' was nevertheless 'not an enemy to it'.[45] This, added to news that his uncle was now 'favourable' to the gospel, must have been a timely piece of encouragement. He was also commanded by the king to use his particular skills to root out some anabaptist sects that were causing concern in Kent and Essex.

However, by the end of the year it was clear that in many quarters Hooper was perceived as something of a destructive troublemaker and a cause of disharmony within the Church. His friend, the cloth merchant John Burcher, writing from Strasbourg, informed Bullinger that 'Hooper is sufficiently comfortable, except that he is not on good terms with the bishop of London'.[46] He then went on to lament the situation and to seek Bullinger to use his considerable influence to resolve the matter:

> This controversy does no little injury to the Christian commonwealth; and the result of the tragedy is expected with some apprehension. The papists are rejoicing at the disagreement between these chief ministers of the word of God, and are hoping that from this controversy the overthrow of the gospel will ensure. Wherefore it would not be out of place, if both parties were reminded of their duty by yourself and the leading preachers of the truth of the present day.

Meanwhile the Council finally took Ridley's side and Hooper was placed under house arrest, forbidden to preach, and permitted only to travel to visit Cranmer, Ridley, or the bishops of Ely or Lincoln, and then only for the purpose of receiving godly advice or to admit his error. Again, Hooper was not cowed by these measures but rather came out fighting. He continued to argue his case, and to that end in December published A godly Confession and Protestacion of the christian faith, made and set forth by Jhon Hooper, wherein is declared what a christian manne is bound to believe of God, hys King, his neibour, and hymselfe.[47]

The purpose of this little book was not to argue the case for abolishing the use of vestments; in fact, vestments were not mentioned even once. 'I protest before God and your majesty', he began, 'I write not this confession for any apology or defence, to contend or strive with any man in any matter, nor for any private affection or displeasure I bear unto any man living, or for any inordinate or partial love unto myself.' Instead, he wished to submit himself and his faith to the scrutiny of the king, Council, and Parliament, and to be judged by them according to the

word of God and in terms of his own testimony and not
swayed by slanderous hearsay. Despite his protestations
to the contrary, the book was in effect a defence. In it he
worked through twenty-one articles of faith to demonstrate
both that he was no heretic or extremist and that the
doctrine he held and preached was the doctrine of the
patriarchs, prophets, and apostles, the primitive church,
and the historic creeds, and not a novelty. As was his
common practice he constantly cited Scripture in his
support; more unusually, he also made many references
to characters and episodes from the worlds of ancient
Greece and Rome. The text was dotted with the names of
Cicero, Aristotle, Scipio, Hannibal, Alexander the Great,
and Julius Caesar and other emperors of Rome, as if,
like Paul addressing the Areopagus at Athens (Acts 17),
Hooper wanted to find an area of common ground with his
audience in addition to using Scripture, and to strive for
men's hearts with more than theology. As always though,
his case ultimately relied on theology, and his conclusion to
the book listed the practical responses that flowed from the
theology. Here the preacher in him took over, and rather
than finishing with a personal, humble confession, he
finished with an exhortation.

It was not an extreme book, either in tone or content.
He had attacked no one personally and, apart from his
customary swipe against negligent ministers, had said little
that could be perceived as contentious. Nevertheless, the
book only served to antagonise the Council more. On 13
January 1551 Hooper was ordered to spend two weeks at
Lambeth Palace in the custody of Cranmer. In spite of the
efforts of the Archbishop, and three meetings with Bucer

and Martyr, he was found to be more obstinate than ever. The Council's patience finally ran out. On 27 January, following a letter from Cranmer, it was decided to commit Hooper to the Fleet prison in London. The following day Martyr wrote to Bullinger:

> And what distresses me most, this dispute has become so vehement, that Hooper is not yet in possession of the bishoprick to which he was appointed, and is excluded from the office of preaching, in which he was employed not without success. God grant that some tranquillity not to be repented of may at length succeed to this turbulent tempest.[48]

The Fleet was known as a debtors' prison and was notorious for the appalling conditions in which the prisoners were kept and for the revolting stench that came from the sewer that ran beside it. Inmates had to pay for their own keep as well as provide their own food and living requirements, or rely on friends or relatives to help them out. Bribing the officials who ran the prison was all but essential if a prisoner was to survive inside. The Fleet 'stood in its own liberty', which meant that it was effectively a law unto itself; neither the mayor nor the sheriffs had much influence over what went on inside its grim walls, and even royal statutes that were intended to improve conditions were generally ignored by the cruel and corrupt gaolers.[49] This, then, was where the Council had sent Hooper in the hope that he would relent.

Only months previously Hooper had rashly declared himself willing to die for his cause, but it was not long before the Council's approach began to bear fruit. The abject conditions in the Fleet no doubt played a large part in softening his stance, but perhaps he had come to the realisation that the eminent Bucer and Martyr were right after all. He wrote one letter that failed to impress the Council. Then on 15 February—following nineteen grim days in prison and the day after Gardiner had finally been deprived of the Winchester bishopric—Hooper wrote a second letter of submission to Cranmer in which he admitted that:

> in this matter I have begun so far to look with suspicion on my own judgment and opinion, that I have considered it more prudent and more becoming Christian humility, to stand and rely on the judgment of your clemency, or of those pious and learned men in the law of God whom you may nominate, than on that of myself alone.[50]

Although he failed to mention vestments by name, speaking instead of 'external things', his letter was contrite enough to secure his release.

On 8 March 1551, less than a month after leaving the Fleet, and nearly a year since the original grant, Hooper was consecrated Bishop of Gloucester at Lambeth Palace by Cranmer, assisted by Ridley and John Ponet, Bishop of Rochester. All were clothed in the legally prescribed vestments. John Foxe later described Hooper's appearance at the ceremony:

> His upper garment was a long scarlet chimere down to the foot, and under that a white linen rochet that covered all his shoulders. Upon his head he had a geometrical, that is, a

four-squared cap, albeit that his head was round. What cause of shame the strangeness hereof was that day to that good preacher every man may easily judge.[51]

Hooper was, however, granted one concession. As a man who, like other Continental reformers, viewed his distinctive long beard as a direct response to the tonsure with its Catholic connotations, he was excused the usual head shaving. He refused to 'become a pie,'[52] as he mockingly put it later.

He took the detailed and convoluted oath, renouncing all papal authority and declaring obedience to the king as supreme head in earth of the Church of England:

> *I, John Hooper, elect bishop of Gloucester, from henceforth shall utterly renounce, refuse, relinquish and forsake the bishop of Rome and his authority, power and jurisdiction, and I shall never consent nor agree that the bishop of Rome shall practice, exercise or have any manner of authority, jurisdiction or power within this realm, or any other the king's dominions, but shall resist the same at all times to the uttermost of my power; and I from henceforth will accept, repute and take the king's majesty to be the only supreme head in earth of the Church of England. And to my cunning, wit and uttermost of my power, without guile, fraud or other undue mean, I will observe, keep, maintain and defend the whole effects and contents of all and singular acts and statutes made and to be made within this realm in derogation, extirpation and extinguishment of the bishop of Rome and his authority, and all other acts and statutes made or to be made in reformation and corroboration in the king's power of the supreme head*

in earth of the Church of England; and this I will do against all manner of persons of what estate, dignity, degree or condition they be, and in no wise do, nor attempt, nor to my power suffer to be done or attempted, directly or indirectly, any thing or things privelie or apartelie, to the let, hindrance, damage or derogation thereof, or any part thereof, by any manner of means or for any manner of pretence; and in case any oath be made, or hath been made, by me to any person or person in maintenance, defence or favour of the bishop of Rome, or his authority, jurisdiction or power, I repute the same as vain and adnichilate, so help me God, all saints and the holy Evangelist.[53]

His Episcopal emblem depicted rays of light pouring down from Heaven upon a lamb in a burning thicket, and his motto was 'Per ignes ad Cœlum'—through the flames to heaven.

John à Lasco and those from the Strangers Church who had so vigorously and committedly championed his cause were understandably disappointed by his apparent capitulation, but others breathed a sigh of relief that a wearisome and damaging episode had finally come to an end.

5

… neither pains untaken,
nor ways unsought

After all the drama and intrigue that culminated in his consecration, Hooper's formal installation at Gloucester, just a fortnight later, was a more low-key affair, with a Cathedral prebendary, John Huntley, officiating. It may have taken many painful and protracted months to reach this moment, but once in possession of the bishopric, Hooper wasted no time in apprising himself of the social and ecclesiastical state of his diocese and setting about addressing what he found. Right from the start it was clear to everyone that he was going to be an energetic, hands-on bishop, zealous in reform—in sharp contrast to his predecessor. He was a bishop, not simply because he had been given that title, but because he did the work of a true bishop and pastor, and set an example to the people. In fact, he was so strenuous in his work that, as early as 3 April, his wife Anna had become concerned enough for his health to tell Bullinger, 'I entreat you to recommend master Hooper to be more moderate in his labour: for he preaches four, or at least three, times a day; and I am afraid lest these over-abundant exertions should cause a premature decay'.[54]

Even before his installation, Hooper had prepared the ground for his reforming work at Gloucester by sending ahead a pastoral letter to all the clergy of the diocese. He wrote to remind them of their high calling, and listed the Scriptural qualities he expected to find in his clergy, challenging them to live by what they professed and preached and so set a godly example to their flocks. In his forthright manner he asked, 'For by what just means canst thou reprehend and blame any other in that fault wherein thou thyself art to be blamed?'

The clergy who received this letter were left in no doubt that their new bishop was an earnest and severe man who took his religion and responsibility very seriously indeed. The letter was, however, only half the message sent by Hooper. Having exhorted the ministers soon to be under his care, he explained, 'And to the intent ye may the more easily perform the same, I have (according to the talent and gift given me of the Lord) collected and gathered out of God's holy word a few articles, which I trust shall much profit and do ye good'. This sounded quite benign, but these 'few articles' turned out to be no less than fifty comprehensive Articles of faith to which every dean, parson, prebend, vicar, curate or other ecclesiastical minister within the diocese had to subscribe. The new

Bishop of Gloucester was determined to run a tight ship, ensuring the affirmation and propagation of reformed doctrine and practice, while also removing anything connected with Roman Catholic superstition.

In addition to the extensive Articles, Hooper also drew up a list of thirty-one Injunctions that he gave to the local ministers during his first visit across the Gloucester diocese. These covered much the same ground as the Articles but had a more personal tone, with a particular emphasis on church discipline and accountability. The new bishop was making it very clear that he was to be regularly informed of what was going on throughout the area for which he had been given responsibility.

Every area of church life was to be ordered and regulated. Public readings from the Prayer Book should be made in English, 'plainly, distinctly, openly, treatably, solemnly, honourably, and devoutly'. If the minister spoke too softly to be heard in all corners of the church, then the whole congregation should be brought into the main body of the building to ensure the people might clearly hear him. This was a practical measure, but also a swipe at the priestly muttering in Latin, which was a feature of the Catholic mass and which particularly offended Protestants. The practice of one neighbour taking Communion on behalf of another—which was common within the diocese—was strictly forbidden. Any minister or parishioner who transgressed the laws of God or the king must be reported to the bishop and face punishment through the Consistory court. No one must be allowed to 'maintain openly or privately, by talking, reading, preaching, disputation, argument, or other reasoning, the defence of transubstantiation of the bread and wine in the sacrament of Christ's precious body and blood.' When broken church windows came to be repaired, no image or picture of any saint was permitted to be painted on the new glass; any such decoration must be 'either branches, flowers, or posies [mottoes] taken out of the holy scripture.'

As if all this was not sufficient, he also drew up a list of twenty-seven Interrogatories and Demands with which clergy should examine their parishioners, and a further list of sixty-one Interrogatories and Examinations with which parishioners might in turn assess their clergy. By this Hooper sought to determine the extent to which his Articles and Injunctions were being adhered to throughout his diocese, and to provide a legalistic mechanism and checklist to identify and exclude the slightest hint of Roman Catholic practice or belief, expose moral transgression, and punish ungodly and unlawful behaviour among the clergy and people alike.[55]

His first visitation around the diocese confirmed his worst suspicions as to the state of the clergy under his care.[56] In fairness, the situation was probably no better or worse than that to be found in most dioceses in England, and the rapidity of religious change was understandably a challenge to clergy who had been used to the old ways. Of three hundred and eleven ministers examined, one hundred and sixty-eight were unable to recite the Ten Commandments from memory, and of those, thirty-one could not say where in Scripture they were to be found. Forty could not say where in scripture the Lord's Prayer could be found and, perhaps worst of all, only nine of those could name its author.

One of the first ministers to fall foul of Hooper's zeal was William Phelps, pastor and curate of Cirencester.[57] He was found to hold Roman Catholic views of the Lord's Supper, but following examination and persuasion by the new bishop he yielded his position with a gushing public submission. This change of heart was undoubtedly due in large part to the power of Hooper's personality and arguments, as well as a desire on Phelps' part to hold on to his living. Given that his new-found beliefs lasted just as long as the rest of Edward's reign and reverted at Mary's accession, he was the proverbial man convinced against his will, who was of the same opinion still.

Likewise, John Wynter, parson of Staunton, was required to repudiate the doctrine of transubstantiation, and on 8 November of that year, in Gloucester cathedral no less, similarly publicly and unequivocally declared:

> *I do with all my heart, being thoroughly persuaded upon good knowledge, long and advised deliberation, without compulsion, fear, and dread, for the truth's sake and contention of mine own conscience, protest, hold, maintain and defend, that in the holy sacrament of Christ's precious body and blood there is no alteration of the substance of bread and wine, but they both do remain in substance very bread and very wine, as well after the words (as they be called) of consecration, as verily as they were bread and wine in substance before… and whosoever be of contrary opinion, and would defend transubstantiation or corporal presence, I do condemn his faith as an error and opinion contrary to the express word of God, and will, with all my learning, wit, diligence, and study, daily improve [disprove], confute, speak*

against, and utterly subvert unto the uttermost of my power,
as God help me in the blood of Christ; to whom with the Holy
Ghost be laud and praise, world without end: so be it. God
save the king.[58]

Wynter too reverted to his former Catholic beliefs as
soon as the religious winds changed direction.

However, Hooper was not without support in his
reforming work in the diocese. His *Godly and most*
necessary Annotations in ye xiii Chapter too the Romaynes,
printed by Thomas Oswen at Worcester in May 1551,[59]
contained a dedication to William Jennings, dean of
Gloucester Cathedral, and John Williams, doctor of the
law and chancellor, whom he described as 'my very loving,
and dear-beloved fellow-labourers in the word of God'. The
book was also dedicated to the ministers of the diocese,
who were exhorted to use it faithfully and regularly for the
spiritual benefit of the people. Hooper signed it, 'Yours
with all my heart, Brother and fellow-preacher, John
Gloucester'. He also received great support and friendship
from two other like-minded men—his chaplain, Guy Eton,
and the rector of Bishop's Cleeve, John Parkhurst—both
of whom were to flee abroad during the persecution of
Protestants in Mary's reign, and from alderman John
Rastell, whom he described as 'a wise and learned man' in
both civil and religious matters.[60]

Hooper's energy and commitment was unquestionable.
John Foxe later testified of him that:

so careful was he in his cure, that he left neither pains
untaken, nor ways unsought, how to train up the flock

of Christ in the true word of salvation... No father in his household, no gardener in his garden, nor husbandman in his vineyard, was more or better occupied, than he in his diocese amongst his flock, going about his towns and villages in teaching and preaching to the people.[61]

Hooper was clearly initially preoccupied with matters of church discipline but was aware too of the economic problems affecting Gloucester. Within a month of arriving in the city he raised a number of concerns with the king's Secretary, William Cecil. Landowners had turned from breeding cattle for meat to rearing sheep for wool, contributing to severe food shortages. The resultant extortionate food prices meant that a 'tyranny of monopoly'[62] allowed some people to profit at the expense of the poor who were going hungry. This had implications for the welfare of individuals and for the stability of the community as a whole. After all, he told his friend, 'You know what a perilous and unruly evil hunger is'.

Profiteering landowners and negligent priests were challenge enough, but as he set about his reforming work in the diocese, Hooper was soon faced with a very different kind of enemy.

6

… the severity of discipline

I n the summer of 1551 Gloucester was struck by a plague known as the 'sweating sickness', which was sweeping across England. This was a particularly virulent and pernicious disease. In London it had killed eight hundred people within the first week of it appearing. John à Lasco's wife and Cranmer's chaplain were both struck down, but survived.[63]

First rearing its ugly head in 1485, it had become so identified with the Tudor period that those who considered the Tudor dynasty to be usurpers to the English throne believed it to be a direct judgement from God. Henry VIII was particularly fearful of it; he regularly moved the royal household out of London into the countryside at the earliest signs of a new epidemic. 'The Sweat', as it was often known, was a highly infectious disease in which the victim suddenly felt unwell, broke out in a profuse sweat, and usually died within three to four hours. Writing to Bullinger in August 1551, Hooper reported that, 'the infection of this disease is in England most severe, and, what is a most remarkable token of divine vengeance, persons are suddenly taken off by it.'[64] In fact, he himself had miraculously recovered from it, but, at the time of writing, Anna and five members of his household had been struck down.

He saw this 'plague of pestilence' as 'God's servant and messenger' to a land and people that deserved God's judgement. He later expressed this view, identifying both causes and remedies, in *An Homily to be read in the time of pestilence*, published in Worcester on 18 March 1553.[65] This was designed for use by the clergy under his care, to warn and instruct the people in the parishes. Hooper was characteristically forthright. 'There is no greater occasion of pestilence than superstition and false religion,' he wrote, 'no greater danger of pestilence than where as the clergy is either ignorant of God's word, or negligent in teaching thereof' and 'nothing provoketh the pestilence more dangerously than where as such sit and be appointed to do justice, do their own affections with contempt and injuries both to God and man.'

Natural medicines had their place in alleviating suffering—Hooper was not against 'the remedies that natural physic hath prescribed'—but what was to him a fundamentally spiritual problem required a spiritual solution, and that was found in Christ and the written word of God.

Even as the sweating sickness[66] was bringing fear and death to Gloucester in the summer of 1551, Hooper continued to preside at the Consistory court which took place in a raised area at the west end of the south aisle of the cathedral. This was a rôle he took very seriously. The court sat more frequently during his bishopric than under any other bishop of Gloucester that century—sometimes daily, usually at Gloucester but elsewhere on occasion. Although he shared duties with other officials—especially John Williams who had been appointed in 1541 under Bishop Wakeman—in his first year he himself presided as judge of over two thirds of the cases brought before the court. Sometimes, if he was absent from Gloucester attending to other duties, cases were delayed until his return. He quickly gained a reputation for treating every case on its merits, and although he had one of those faces that was severe by nature, and could be harsh when he felt it was necessary, he could also demonstrate compassion, flexibility, and imagination. He regularly attempted to resolve family disputes out of court, by acting as an arbitrator rather than a formal judge. It was clear, however, that he could be an intimidating figure, and even his friends felt he was sometimes a little severe. Martin Micron, writing to Bullinger on 7 November 1551, said of Hooper, 'Let him be exhorted to unite prudence and Christian lenity to the severity of discipline.'[67]

Being an ecclesiastical court rather than a secular one (although jurisdiction inevitably over-lapped from time to time) the offences dealt with by the Consistory court related to the 'health of the soul', and the punishment meted out by Hooper consisted of various forms of penance. This was not simply a private matter, but a very public one. The convicted wrongdoer was dressed in a white shirt and sheet, and standing barefoot and bareheaded was required to openly confess his or her offences before the local congregation and often also at prominent public places and on the busiest days—market days—with an 'apparitor' appointed by the court observing the penance being done. Hooper had dispensed with the added requirement under Wakeman of holding a lighted candle and reciting the Lord's Prayer. On occasions, however, the penitents were placed in a 'whyche' or cell at the high cross at the centre of Gloucester, dressed in the usual white apparel, with a notice of their offence on their forehead and a requirement for them to announce it to all who passed by.

One penitent, John Parry of Brockworth, was required to announce standing upon the high cross, that 'this penance I am commanded to do for that I have committed adultery with a woman whom upon mine oath before I declared to be an honest woman, and in like manner six Sundays following in the parish church of Brockworth'. Joan Vynche of Pauntley had to do penance for three days both in Newent market place and in her parish church. Having been found guilty of adultery, Thomas Hudson did penance at Gloucester cross, Gloucester cathedral, and locations in Tewkesbury, Cirencester, and Berkeley. However, Hooper took pity on Elizabeth Piers, alias Tilar, who had been convicted of adultery with a 'John'; she was pardoned and dismissed on the grounds that her husband had left her with three children for another woman nine years before and her only child by 'John' had died.

Hooper condemned the bribery and corruption that was rife within both secular and ecclesiastical court systems. His judgements were never swayed by financial inducements. Writing some time later, he commented on such abuses and the injustice that resulted, declaring that, 'daily it is seen in every consistory court, that, at the will and pleasure of a wicked man that is the bishop's officer, the innocents be cursed, and used worse than dogs, until such time as the officer's fury be pacified with gold of silver'.

Hooper was likewise not swayed by a person's prominence or rank. John ab Ulmis, Bullinger's young protégé, writing to his former mentor in Zurich on 4 December 1551, reported that some people had accused Hooper of 'acting with severity in the discharge of his function towards tradespeople and those of the lower orders but lax and indulgent towards those of higher rank'.[68] Hooper's response to these allegations, he reported, was to declare indignantly, 'My brethren, I wish you would bring before me any of the chief nobility, whom you can prove by positive evidence to have been guilty either of fornication or adultery, and you may punish me with death if I fail to convince you of the impartiality of my proceedings towards all alike'.[69] This was soon evidenced by his dealings with Sir Anthony Kingston, the man who had been instrumental in crushing the West Country rebellion. Kingston was a wealthy landowner with many estates in Gloucestershire, and was a prominent member of the Council for the Welsh Marches. He also had royal connections since his father had been a member of Henry VIII's Privy Chamber and keeper of the Tower of London, and his mother had been a lady-in-waiting to Anne Boleyn in the Tower. An accusation of adultery was made against Kingston and he was ordered to appear before the

Consistory court. Initially he simply, arrogantly refused. When he eventually condescended to attend Hooper rebuked him. Kingston responded by publicly abusing the bishop before striking him on the cheek. This added a serious civil offence to the accusation of adultery. Hooper was in regular contact still with the Privy Council through his friend Secretary William Cecil, and reported the matter immediately. As a result, Kingston was fined the not inconsiderable sum of five hundred pounds for the assault, and still had to face Hooper again for sentence on the charge of adultery. 'There is no man more privileged than the other', Hooper had once written. 'As justice is executed against the inferior, so should it be against the superior; for as one is subject unto the law of God, so is the other'.

Hooper's diocesan activities alone would have been more than enough for most men, but he was also very involved in the House of Lords and sometimes stayed with Cranmer at Lambeth Palace while he was in London. His commitment to the work of parliament was recognised in April 1553 when he was rewarded for his services with the sum of twenty pounds.[70] Meanwhile, his ecclesiastical star had been rising since the resolution of the vestments controversy and his installation at Gloucester, and on 6 October 1551 he was included as one of eight bishops appointed to a commission established to carry out a reform of canon law, along with eight divines, eight civil lawyers, and eight canon lawyers; John à Lasco, Peter Martyr, Justice Sir James Hales, Hugh Latimer, Bishop Ridley and William Cecil were among his colleagues.[71] Still further responsibilities and a new appointment were not far away.

7

… content yourself with patience[72]

The traditionalist Bishop of Worcester, Nicholas Heath, had been appointed to a commission engaged to prepare a new Ordinal to replace the one to which Hooper had so objected. In actual fact, Cranmer had already done most of the preparation himself, so that the commission was something of a rubber-stamp exercise. The tone of this new book was strongly Protestant, and when, early in 1550, the time came for the twelve commissioners to put their names to it, Heath alone refused to sign. Following a hearing before the Privy Council on 4 March 1550, he was committed to the Fleet. After a year and a half in prison he still refused to subscribe. On 24 October 1551 he was duly deprived of his bishopric, and the office of Bishop of Worcester fell vacant.

In a hint of things to come, Peter Martyr, writing to

Bullinger two days later, expressed his admiration for Hooper, whom he had met just before Easter at Oxford:

> *the probity of this bishop, and his zeal for religion, together with the long intimacy that has existed between us, and, lastly, your especial commendation of him, (which has very great weight with me, as it ought to have) render him an object of my peculiar regard: wherefore you need not doubt but that I shall exert myself in his favour to the utmost of my power.*[73]

At the same time as the process of Heath's deprivation was drawing to a close, the rehabilitated Duke of Somerset was once more in deep trouble. Charged with treason and felony, he was arrested and placed in the Tower. With unseemly haste he was brought to trial and sentenced to death for felony. Despite the strenuous efforts of Cranmer and Ridley, he was finally beheaded on 22 January 1552. In a last-minute act of mercy he was—like Anne Boleyn—granted the expert services of an executioner brought from France.

Another former patron of Hooper, Sir Thomas Arundel, was implicated in Somerset's crime and soon also went to the scaffold.

The continuing vacancy at Worcester following Heath's deprivation was soon having an unsettling effect on the diocese. This was highlighted in the New Year when the Bishop's Palace was raided. On 24 January 1552 a letter was sent by a concerned Council to the Dean and Chapter of Worcester ordering them to take steps 'as well for the recovery of that hath been spoiled of the late Bishop of

Worcester's house as also for the safe custody of such things as are still remaining there'. The identity of the raiders was not known but suspicion quickly fell on supporters of Heath exacting revenge for his removal and imprisonment. On 29 January the Council fired off a warning to an un-named individual not to do any more damage to the Bishop's Palace either at Heath's request or on Heath's behalf. There was clearly an urgent need to fill the vacancy. At the same time, Martin Micron noted that, 'The authority of master Hooper in the council is daily increasing, whence the greatest benefit, I hope, will accrue to the church'.[74] The Earl of Warwick, another admirer of Hooper, expressed concern that such a respected man should have to make do with a poor bishopric like Gloucester. Finally, on 20 March, Cranmer could inform Bullinger that, 'master Hooper is in such great esteem among us, that he is now appointed bishop of Worcester'.[75]

As it turned out, the exact method for putting the appointment into effect was less than straightforward. On 26 April Hooper surrendered the Gloucester bishopric to the king. Letters Patent confirming his appointment to Worcester were issued on 20 May, while at the same time Gloucester was dissolved as a separate diocese and combined with Worcester. Having been enthroned by proxy on 18 June, he immediately began a visitation of his new diocese, using the Articles and Injunctions he had drawn up for Gloucester. Within days of arriving, however, he had to return urgently to Gloucester when he received news of the 'negligence and ungodly behaviour'[76] of the ministers there. It seemed to him that whenever he was away from Gloucester for any length of time the ministers took advantage of his absence to revert to old habits. In an attempt to address this situation he appointed a number of superintendents throughout the diocese to keep an eye on things on his behalf. He was so preoccupied during this time that some of his friends complained amongst themselves that he was too busy to write to them.

During this brief return to Gloucester Hooper was mostly concerned with the local clergy, but he also found time to write to William Cecil. He offered his usual mix of news and advice, openly confessing present difficulties and alerting the king's Secretary to certain impending issues. However, he closed the letter with warm words of concern for his 'singular friend'. 'Your health is not the surest: favour it as ye may', he wrote, 'and charge it not too far. Ye be wise and comfortable for others; be so for yourself also'.[77] Then, knowing how Cecil's duties often weighed heavy on him, Hooper encouraged him to keep trusting God even when things didn't seem to work out as planned or hoped. 'When even your best intentions go wrong', he wrote, 'content yourself with patience'.[78]

On his return to Worcester, Hooper was soon in need of great patience himself as he encountered resistance to change among the clergy there too. In particular, two canons of the cathedral, Henry Joliffe and Robert Johnson, refused to subscribe to the Articles of faith. Both men had been at the cathedral for a number of years—Joliffe since 1541 and Johnson since 1544. Being conservatives in doctrine and practice they were supporters of their former bishop, Heath, and were no doubt still smarting at the way in which he had been treated. Furthermore, Johnson had overseen the administration of the Worcester diocese during the period of vacancy and naturally resented the fact that Hooper brought in his own officials to run things under the new régime. Following a public debate with these two 'loose' rebel canons, Hooper sent a report to the Council, which in turn sent two representatives, Cheke and Harley, to investigate the matter. A clearly frustrated Hooper, writing again to Secretary Cecil on 25 October, told his dear friend, 'Ah, Mr Secretary, that there were good men in the cathedral churches! God then should have much more honour than he hath, the king's majesty more obedience, and the poor people more knowledge'.[79]

As he had done in Gloucester, Hooper continued to set an example by putting his beliefs into action. John Foxe was struck by Hooper's blend of practical and spiritual concern for the poor:

> I was twice, as I remember, in his house at Worcester, where, in his common hall, I saw a table spread with good store of meat, and beset full of beggars and poor folk; and I asking his servants what this meant, they told me that every day their lord and master's manner was to have to dinner a certain number of poor folk of the city in turns, who were served by four at a mess, with wholesome meats; and when they were served (being previously examined by him or his deputies in the Lord's prayer, the articles of their faith, and ten commandments) then he himself sat down to dinner, and not before.[80]

The mechanics of Hooper's new appointment were not finalised until the end of the year. At last, on 8 December, the bishoprics of Worcester and Gloucester were re-established as separate entities and Hooper was appointed to both by Letters Patent. His formal enthronement at Worcester took place just five days before Christmas, and the intention was that he would spend six months in each diocese per year. As it turned out, any plans he had were soon overtaken by events unfolding elsewhere.

Portrait of Ioannes Hooperus

© Gloucester City Museum and Art Gallery.

St Mary's Gateway

© Pete Sullivan

Gloucester Folk Museum,
traditionally known as Bishop Hooper's lodging
© Pete Sullivan

Philip and Mary Coin
courtesy of Antony Wilson at York Coins. www.yorkcoins.com

The Hooper statue within the Monument

© Pete Sullivan

The Hooper Monument, St Mary's Square

© Pete Sullivan.

The Burning of Master Hooper, Bishop of Gloucester from John Foxe's Acts and Monuments ed. Rev. G Townsend 1846 edition.

8

… by reason of our sins

When Hooper preached before the king towards the end of February 1553 it must have been evident to him that the rumours circulating concerning Edward's poor health were well founded. The king's illness was certainly serious enough for questions of the royal succession to be raised.[81] Henry VIII's will, with the full weight of an Act of Parliament behind it, decreed that, should Edward die, the crown should pass to Mary, Henry's daughter by Katherine of Aragon. The Duke of Northumberland—as the Earl of Warwick was now titled—viewed this prospect as a Catholic threat to Protestantism, and devised a plan, not only to preserve the reforms of Edward's brief reign but also to secure his own position and power. He and the frail Edward sought to prevent Mary's accession by a document known as the 'King's Device', by which the crown would pass to Lady Jane

Grey and her male heirs. In fact, the Device was originally designed to exclude any *female* succession and had spoken simply of Lady Jane's male heirs, until the king changed it on his deathbed. Jane Grey was certainly of royal blood since her mother, Frances Brandon, was the daughter of Mary, younger sister of Henry VIII. Jane's mother was still alive at this time and had to be persuaded into passing any claim to the throne she herself had to her daughter. Northumberland sought to strengthen his own position by arranging for Jane to marry Guildford Dudley, one of his sons.

Northumberland then managed to persuade the members of the Privy Council to put their names to a second document agreeing to uphold the Device. However, he found the judges and legal officers—who were also required to sign—harder to bring on board. They had deep reservations about the legality of the plan, believing that the Act of Parliament giving the crown to Mary could only be repealed by another Act of Parliament. However, they finally buckled in the face of Northumberland's coercion, and all but one judge signed the second document. The one exception was Justice Sir James Hales whose legal scruples were later to result in his imprisonment in the Fleet under Mary and whose subsequent suffering in prison was to come to the particular notice of Hooper.

Writing from London on 7 June 1553, John Utenhove, John à Lasco's Flemish co-worker at the Strangers Church, explained to Bullinger:

> *We have no news, except that the king, who has lately been in the most imminent danger from a most severe cough,*

*which had already attacked his inside even to the very vitals,
is now somewhat better, though it is hardly possible that
his health will be entirely restored during the whole of this
summer.*[82]

The king's Secretary and Hooper's friend, William Cecil, was also unwell at that time and received a letter from Lord Audley which not only offered hearty encouragement but prescribed a sure-fire remedy for any weakness or consumption:

*Flay and quarter a nine day old sow, put in a still with a
handful of spearmint, one of red fennel, one of liverwort,
half a handful of turnip, a handful of celery, nine clean picked
and pared dates, a handful of great raisins, stoned, ¼ oz of
mace and two sticks of cinnamon pressed in a mortar. Distil
with soft fire; set in a glass in the sun nine days, and drink
nine spoonfuls at once when you wish. A compost. Quarter a
hedgehog, and put in a still with a quart of red wine, a pint of
rose water, a quart of sugar, cinnamon and great raisins, one
date, twelve neeps.*[83]

Lord Audley had great confidence in his potions. 'Tell me of any disease you have', he told Cecil in conclusion, 'and I will send you a proved remedy'.

Cecil may or may not have followed this advice, but he certainly recovered from his sickness. As for the young king, no remedy could be found.

Edward died at Greenwich on 6 July 1553, and England entered a period of uncertainty, turmoil, and—in some cases—retribution and revenge.

The rumour-mill went into overdrive as various reports circulated as to what, or whom, had brought about Edward's death. According to Julius Trentian, another Protestant correspondent, writing to Bullinger some months later, the king had died 'of consumption, as the physicians assert; by poison, according to common report'.[84] Some blamed Catholic plotters, while others saw the scheming hand of Northumberland at work.

Lady Jane Grey was immediately proclaimed queen when she arrived in London four days later. Mary went to Kenninghall, Norfolk, and there proclaimed *herself* queen. On 9 July she wrote to the Council to assert her right to the throne.

The Council's response, dated the same day, was as clear as it was swift. First, Lady Jane Grey was declared 'our Sovereign Lady Queen Jane' on the grounds that she was:

> *invested and possessed with right and just title in the Imperial Crown of this Realm, not only by good order of old ancient laws of this realm, but also by your late Sovereign Lord's [Edward's] letters patent signed with his own hand and sealed with the Great Seal of England in the presence of the most part of the nobles and councillors, judges, and diverse other grown and sage persons assenting and subscribing unto the same.*[85]

Second, according to 'the everlasting law of God', the considered opinion of 'the notable and learned universities of Christendom', and 'diverse acts of parliament', Mary was declared illegitimate on account of the annulment of Henry VIII's marriage to her mother, Katherine of Aragon.

Consequently, the Council called on Mary to drop her pretensions to the Crown and demonstrate her obedience and allegiance to queen Jane. Those who signed the letter, describing themselves as Mary's 'loving friends', no doubt hoped she would submit. Within days events would prove they had underestimated Mary and misjudged the mood of the people.

On the same day as these letters were being exchanged, Bishop Ridley preached a sermon at Paul's Cross in London in which he spoke in support of Lady Jane Grey and warned that should Mary become queen, not only would all the reforms under Edward be undone but England risked coming under the control of a foreign, Catholic power—Spain. His comments were highly perceptive, but in the circumstances also somewhat reckless.

On hearing of Edward's death, Hooper, by contrast, put his belief in the doctrine of Christian obedience above even his deep hatred of Catholicism. Mary may have been a papist but, to him, she was also the lawful sovereign. Accordingly, he called on the people of Gloucestershire and Worcestershire to take Mary's side, and personally rode from place to place 'to win and stay the people for her party'.[86] Furthermore, he gave instructions to requisition horses to be sent to aid Mary who had gone from Kenninghall to Framlingham Castle in Suffolk.

The power-struggle for the throne did not last long. Support for Mary was strengthening among the common people and landowners alike. Not surprisingly, those who had been closet-Catholics during Edward's reign quickly rallied to her cause, but Protestants too took her side; there were some, like Hooper, who did so for the sake of law and obedience, but others, like many in Suffolk, who not only hated Northumberland's arrogance but had apparently received assurances from Mary that she would not go back on the religious changes that had been made under her brother, despite her own publicly-held Catholic convictions.

In an attempt to put pressure on Mary, Northumberland sought to confront her with a mercenary army, but this failed miserably. With Northumberland absent from London and his fortunes sinking as rapidly as Mary's were rising, the Council at last recognised where the momentum lay and changed their allegiance. Hooper's friend, William Cecil, was duly sent to make a somewhat grovelling declaration of loyalty to Mary. Those surrounding Queen Jane were still trying desperately to secure her position and sent letters to a number of knights, including Sir Anthony Kingston, to prepare forces to suppress any rebellion against her. But it was too late. On 19 July the Lord Mayor of London proclaimed Mary queen, much to the joy of the people. At Gloucester a trumpeter supplied by Sir John Brydges heralded the proclamation. Recognising how events were moving, Northumberland himself submitted at Cambridge before being arrested and taken to the Tower of London. Within a month he was condemned for high treason and beheaded, having apparently returned to the Catholic fold and from the scaffold exhorted others to follow his example.

Bishop Ridley also submitted to Mary but was arrested and placed in the Tower. Mary was not prepared to overlook his Paul's Cross pronouncements, and in any case she eagerly desired the restoration of Bonner to the London bishopric.

On 3 August a suitably dressed and bejewelled Mary entered London with her supporters to be greeted by the people. Gardiner was released from the Tower, restored as Bishop of Winchester in place of John Ponet, and appointed to the high office of Lord Chancellor, This was just the beginning of a series of ecclesiastical tables that would be turned in the subsequent weeks and months. Miles Coverdale was removed as Bishop of Exeter and replaced by John Veysey; George Day replaced John Scory at Chichester; John Hooper was soon deprived of the bishopric of Worcester and Nicholas Heath reappointed.

Bonner was released from the Marshalsea on 5 August, and on the same day Edward Underhill, 'Hooper's champion', was arrested for publishing an anti-Catholic ballad and sent to Newgate prison. Underhill proved to be one of the great survivors of this turbulent period. He gained favour with the keeper of Newgate by playing his lute and singing at dinner. Following a period of illness, he was released from prison. He managed to hold fast to his Protestant beliefs and still remain loyal to the queen, finally retiring to the countryside near Coventry.

Edward's funeral at Westminster Abbey on 8 August 1553 not only marked the death of the sovereign but also symbolised the passing of the Protestant régime and the ushering in of the return to Catholicism. Archbishop Cranmer—who was still in office despite putting his name to the Council's rejection of Mary's pretensions to the throne—officiated using the Protestant Prayer Book of 1552, and the sermon, delivered by the reappointed

Catholic Bishop Day of Chichester, was a clear sign of things to come. Mary herself chose not to lend her presence to the occasion but instead attended a requiem mass at the Tower, with Stephen Gardiner officiating.

The anti-Protestant backlash was gathering pace and Hooper of all people understood the very real danger he was in. He was soon to inform Bullinger: 'Our king is taken from us by reason of our sins... We now place our confidence in God alone, and earnestly entreat him to comfort and strengthen us to endure any sufferings whatever for the Glory of His name.'[87]

9

… once I did flee

During the reign of Henry VIII Hooper had escaped abroad to avoid persecution under the Six Articles of 1539. While engaged at the home of Sir Thomas Arundel, he had borrowed a horse from a friend whom he had saved from the gallows, and then had made his way to the coast. From there he had sailed to France, spending a brief time in Paris and Strasbourg before returning to England. It was not long before he was compelled to flee again; on that occasion he pretended to be the captain of a ship sailing to Ireland and crossed to France once more before travelling on to Strasbourg, and then Basle, where he and Anna de Tserclas married in late March 1547.[88] Now, under Mary, he faced fleeing again. Other leading Protestants, including John Ponet, John Knox, and John Foxe, escaped abroad illegally—that is, without having a passport granted by the government—and

Protestant fishermen on the Sussex coast were willing to risk providing transport across the Channel.[89] This time, however, Hooper decided he must remain in England and face the consequences. 'Once I did flee', he said, 'but now, because I am called to this vocation, I am thoroughly persuaded to tarry, and to live and die with my sheep'.[90] Soon after leaving Zurich in 1549 he had told Bullinger, almost prophetically:

> Let others talk, and extenuate and make what excuse they please, who, when the wolf is coming have left their sheep to be torn in pieces by thieves and robbers: unless they repent, they will wretchedly suffer the punishment of hirelings in that day when the true Shepherd shall come to separate the sheep from the goats.[91]

He was certainly no hireling. God had given him a flock (or two) to guard, and to desert them now would be a repudiation of his calling and a dereliction of his duty. He was, however, not only a bishop; he was also a husband and a father and so had responsibilities and duties towards his family too. For now, Anna and Rachel, and a new son, Daniel, would remain in England, but the time would come when Hooper would feel compelled to send them to comparative safety abroad.

On 22 August 1553, while at Gloucester, Hooper received a demand for his 'undelayed repair unto the Court where to attend upon the lords of the Council'. He must have been anticipating such a summons. Having sat for the last time at the Consistory court at Gloucester on 26 August, he duly travelled to London. Arriving in the city, he expected to appear before Bishop Heath and the recently released Bishop Bonner, but on 29 August he was taken instead to appear before Mary and her Council at Richmond, apparently to answer extraordinary charges that he owed money to the queen. (In a letter of 7 January 1554 Hooper later contended that in fact it was Mary who owed *him* the sum of £80 or more on account of his being deprived of his bishoprics and the income due from them).[92] Undoubtedly he had been summoned because he was known to be an heretical ringleader. Technically, however, he could not face religious charges since the Protestant reforms were still legally in place and Catholic practices such as the mass were still illegal. Despite this, Gardiner—who was no doubt relishing his restoration to favour and power—took the opportunity to taunt him about his religious doctrines, but Hooper boldly stood his ground. When proceedings had drawn to a close on 1 September, he was committed to the Fleet.

Writing to Bullinger from prison on 3 September Hooper relayed his sad news and detailed the sudden changes that had taken place. 'The altars are again set up throughout the kingdom', he lamented, 'private masses are frequently celebrated in many quarters; the true worship of God, true invocation, the right use of the sacraments, are all done away with; divine things are trodden underfoot, and human things have the pre-eminence'. True preachers of the gospel were in grave danger, he explained, and 'those who have not yet known by experience the filthiness of a prison, are hourly looking for it'.[93]

Bullinger was already aware of recent events in England, and was greatly distressed by them. 'Oh! how truly wretched are the times into which our good Lord has thought fit for us to enter!' he told John Calvin's colleague at Geneva, Theodore Beza. 'Let us earnestly implore his mercy,' he continued, 'that he may shew pity upon us and upon his most afflicted church.'[94]

Early in September, Archbishop Cranmer took the fateful step of making a public declaration repudiating the Catholic mass and defending the legal status of the Prayer Book. He had planned to issue it by having copies bearing his official seal nailed to every church door in London. As it turned out his plans were pre-empted by a friend who took it upon himself to publish a draft of the declaration. It was soon widely circulated throughout the city, encouraging Protestants and incurring the displeasure of the new régime. Within days he faced members of Mary's Council, including Bishops Gardiner and Heath, and when he refused to repudiate the declaration he was sent to the Tower, finding himself in the very same chamber in which the Duke of Northumberland had prepared for execution.

While Hooper languished in the Fleet, and other Protestant leaders were imprisoned elsewhere, the rest of London prepared to celebrate Mary's coronation,[95] and on 30 September Mary rode through the city in a beautifully decorated, canopied carriage drawn by six finely apparelled horses. In front of her rode Gardiner and other dignitaries including the Mayor of London. Behind her, in a carriage decorated with cloth of silver, came her half-sister Elizabeth and Anne of Cleves. All along the route the procession was greeted by elaborate and costly pageants, and the city's water conduits ran with wine. The next day Mary was crowned and anointed by Gardiner.

The ceremony was long and followed Catholic rites; clear evidence of the rapid return to Catholicism and the firm repudiation of all things Protestant.

Further evidence of the extent of this return and repudiation came in Gardiner's opening speech to Mary's first parliament, convened on 5 October, in which he dropped veiled hints of a possible reunion with Rome although there was no mention of the papacy itself so soon. By the time parliament was dissolved on 5 December it had repealed all of the Protestant reforms of Edward's reign, paving the way for the seemingly inevitable restoration of England to papal jurisdiction. Mary herself was certainly looking towards that goal. Back in August she had secretly received two papal envoys; one on behalf of the exiled Cardinal Pole, and the other, Gian Francesco Commendone, reporting directly back to Pope Julius III himself.[96]

Meanwhile, conditions for Hooper were going from bad to worse. The warden at the time of his imprisonment was a man named Babington, who treated him unjustly and harshly. Babington had friends in very high places and regularly called on the backing of Gardiner in the vindictive treatment of his prisoner. Despite paying the sum of £5 to have liberty of the prison right from the start, Hooper was put in solitary confinement in the tower chamber. After three months he was permitted to take some of his meals with fellow prisoners but not allowed to converse with them. Babington and his wife—whom Hooper described as 'a wicked man and woman'—used these meal times as an opportunity to pick quarrels with him. When the subject turned to the contentious issue of the mass, the warden reported back to Gardiner and obtained permission to make life even harder for Hooper, who was subsequently placed in a room with a bed consisting simply of 'a little pad of straw and a rotten covering with a tick and a few feathers therein'. As a concession, and probably in return for an appropriate sum, Babington permitted some friends of Hooper to supply fresh bedding.

The abject conditions, combined with the stench from the city sewer that was all too familiar to him from his previous stay in the Fleet, resulted in Hooper becoming seriously ill, to the point that he quite expected to die in that place before he ever faced a trial. On occasions when he was in particular distress he called out for help, but Babington refused to permit anyone to go to his aid, saying cruelly, 'Let him alone; it were a good riddance of him'. Bullinger too expected the worst. Writing to Calvin on 15 October he spoke of Hooper as one 'whom I suspect by this time to have been removed from this world'.[97]

Like other leading Protestants imprisoned elsewhere, Hooper put his energies into writing letters and more extensive works whenever strength, circumstances and resources permitted, but it was never easy for him to maintain any kind of correspondence. In the first place, the actual process of writing had to be done secretly; one letter to John à Lasco, dated 25 November of that year, was written 'in haste and by stealth from prison'.[98] Then, even if a letter managed to be smuggled out it regularly didn't reach its destination, often due to plain treachery or untrustworthy couriers. No wonder Hooper later confessed to Bullinger: 'I would write more openly, if I dared; but I

9   ... *once I did flee*   101

have often been deceived by my friends.'[99] Likewise, Hooper never received a good number of letters sent to him, mostly for the same reasons.

Hooper's principal contact with the outside world was his 'faithful servant', William Downton, who was an almost constant companion to him in the Fleet. Downton was also the regular conduit through which Hooper sent and received letters and other writings; a fact that was evidently not lost on Babington and the other gaolers. On one visit he was strip-searched and ended up being detained himself even though no letters were found. The search did, however, uncover a list of the names of some of Hooper's supporters that was duly passed on to Gardiner for further action—something that understandably concerned Hooper a great deal.

On 13 October Hooper wrote to Anna, his 'dearly beloved and my godly wife', as he described her. In truth, the letter was more of a sermon than a personal message, perhaps because he knew that it would inevitably have a wider readership than just his wife. It was long and full of encouragement, comfort, and exhortation, but there was little warmth or intimacy in it. Apart from the opening, he only addressed Anna three times more in the whole letter and never once by name. His priority, as always was not to express human affection but to expound the word of God.

In the face of this unjust persecution he recognised what God had commanded as a response:

> *Seeing therefore that we live for this life amongst so many and great perils and dangers, we must be well assured by God's word how to bear them, and how patiently to take*

them, as they be sent to us from God. We must also assure ourselves that there is no other remedy for Christians in the time of trouble than Christ himself hath appointed us. In St Luke [21.19] he giveth us this commandment: "Ye shall possess your lives in patience" saith he. In the which words he giveth us both commandment what to do, and also great comfort and consolation in all troubles ... he biddeth us be patient, and in no case violently nor seditiously to resist our persecutors, because God hath such cure and charge of us, that he will keep in the midst of all troubles the very hairs of our head, so that one of them shall not fall away without the will and pleasure of our heavenly Father.

This patience was not the sort that derives from the intellect or the emotions—after all, Hooper himself had always been impatient for religious change, for example—it was, as he had once told Secretary Cecil, the patience born of a deep faith and trust in God. In a moment of faith combined with a rare hint of vulnerability he wrote:

We may suffer things, and feel them as mortal men; yet bear them, and overcome them as christian men. We may be attempted of the devil, the flesh, and the world; but yet although these things pinch, they do not pierce.

He wanted his wife to be consoled by the word of God and above all to remain patient and submitted to God's will. He concluded:

So doth the merciful Father lay upon us now imprisonment (and, I suppose, for my part shortly death), now spoil of goods, loss of friends, and, the greatest loss of all, the knowledge of God's word. God's will be done!

He signed off, 'Your brother in Christ'.[100]

The preacher in him had not been removed by imprisonment, even if he now had to express himself on paper rather than in a pulpit. The pastor in him was also undiminished. When his godly wisdom was sought he was ready to offer it.

Hooper wrote a note to a 'mistress Wilkinson'—Joan Wilkinson, a widow from King's Stanley in Gloucestershire whom he had known during his time as bishop—to thank her for the 'loving tokens' she had sent him. He also took the opportunity to encourage her to continue in her faith and to 'rejoice in such troubles as shall happen unto you for the truth's sake: for in that part Christ saith you be happy'. She should know, he told her, that it was better to adhere to the truth and be in a minority with God's people than to follow the majority in its error. Her faithful support of imprisoned Protestants extended also to Oxford where Cranmer, Ridley and Hugh Latimer were being held. As a result of Cranmer's advice in a letter to her, she eventually decided to flee England to join Anna Hooper and other refugees at Frankfurt. She died there in 1556, and in her will left twenty pounds for the education of Daniel Hooper.

Likewise, Hooper thanked another courageous Protestant woman, Ann Warcop, addressed as 'mistress A.W.', for her 'loving token', praised her for her constant faith, and exhorted her, saying, 'Sister, take heed: you shall in your journey towards heaven meet with many a monstrous beast; have salve of God's word therefore ready'.

To a London merchant who had supported him in prison he expressed deep gratitude and offered passionate encouragement to always test truth and falsehood by the word of God. To another group of supporters in London he wrote heartfelt thanks:

> I have received from you, dearly beloved in our Saviour Jesus Christ, by the hands of my servant, William Downton, your liberality, for the which I do most heartily thank you; and I praise God highly in you and for you, who hath moved your hearts to shew this kindness towards me; praying him to preserve you from all famine, scarcity, and lack of the truth of his word, which is the lively food of your souls, as you preserve my body from hunger and other necessities which should happen unto me, were it not cared for by the benevolence and charity of godly people.

He had warm words for John Hall and his wife who had demonstrated such 'loving and gentle friendship' towards him, assuring them of his prayers for them, and in turn humbly seeking theirs for him.

When he heard that a previously zealous Protestant had, 'through the devilish persuasions and wicked counsel of worldly men', gone back on his faith, he was desperately saddened. In previous times he would have sought to persuade the man face to face, but now he had to accomplish it by letter. His tone was firm but compassionate. Like the illustrious penitents of Scripture, this man too could know God's love and mercy:

> Acknowledge your offence, and from whence ye are fallen

… Mourn with Mary Magdalen, lament with David, cry with Jonas, and weep with Peter; and make no tarrying to turn to the Lord, whose pitiful eyes attend always to wipe away the tears from every troubled conscience.

In the face of 'pestilent persuasions' and 'antichrist's tyranny' the answer was never to cave in, he told the man; the choice must be either to 'fly this wicked realm'—he wouldn't be alone in taking that course of action—or, following Hooper's own example, 'with boldness of heart and patience of the spirit bear manfully the cross even unto the death'.

Former Bishop of London, Nicholas Ridley, was also a prolific writer while imprisoned in the Tower and later at Oxford. His confinement, plus the powerful common bond created by the ongoing persecution, gave him a new perspective on the controversy over vestments he had fought with Hooper. He had already received two letters from Hooper but had been unable to reply immediately. Now, in a warm, conciliatory letter, he addressed his old adversary as 'my dearly beloved brother and fellow-elder' and admitted:

for as much as I understand by your former works, which I have yet but superficially seen, that we thoroughly agree and wholly consent together in those things which are the grounds and substantial points of our religion, against which the world so furiously rageth in these our days; howsoever in time past, in smaller matters and circumstances of religion, your wisdom and my simplicity (I confess) have in some points varied; now, I say, be you assured, that even with my whole heart, God is my witness, in the bowels of Christ, I love you in the truth, and for the truth's sake which abideth in us, and, I am persuaded, shall, by the grace of God, abide in us for evermore.[101]

Such words must have been a source of great encouragement and joy to Hooper, but they had no power to change the events that were unfolding.

10

… till death unmarry me

Even before the crown had been placed on Mary's head, thoughts in royal circles had turned to securing a Catholic succession; that required Mary, who was now thirty-seven and rarely in the best of health, to have a child, which in turn demanded of her that she be married.

From the word go, the Emperor Charles V, Mary's cousin, employed his ambassadors in England to manoeuvre his son, Philip of Spain, into serious contention for Mary's hand. He was fully aware that the queen's marriage to a Spanish prince might prove unpopular—'loathed as all foreigners are by all Englishmen'[102]—but was determined to pursue the matter. First, however, he had to quickly scupper tentative marriage negotiations between Philip and the Portuguese Infanta, Maria. This was successfully accomplished, albeit with some unfortunate offence to the

Portuguese royal family. Through the skills of the Imperial ambassador, Simon Renard, Mary was soon coming round to the idea of marrying Philip and by the end of October 1553 was privately expressing her determination in that direction. When the Privy Council was formally informed on 8 November, it was clear that the queen's mind was fully made up, and even opponents of the match, like Gardiner, or others who had misgivings, dared not express opposition. Despite a call from some in parliament for Mary to marry within England, deliberations got under way to draw up two treaties for the marriage to Philip; the first, to provide for the succession, and the second, to place conditions and safeguards on Philip's future rôle. Such agreements were essential for everyone involved on a practical level, but were also an attempt to allay the growing fears of a Spanish take-over of England. On 7 December the Council accepted the treaties but the public declaration of all the details on 14 January 1554 merely served to stir the already simmering public unease and discontent.

A co-ordinated plan of widespread rebellion was secretly drawn up by some parts of the nobility, and was set to break out in the middle of March. As it turned out, the plot was exposed at the end of January and the rebels' hand was forced. Of those areas expected to be involved, only Kent took any significant action. A force of around 3,000 men, under the leadership of Sir Thomas Wyatt, managed to get as far as the Thames at Southwark on 3 February, ransacking Gardiner's home and destroying his personal library. Without the full support of the citizens of London, however, the rebellion fizzled out on 7 February, Ash

Wednesday. Just days later Gardiner preached a Lenten sermon before the queen in which he declared that, for the sake of the whole realm, those who were intent on rebellion must be removed immediately before their treachery and treason could spread. On Monday 12 February Lady Jane Grey's husband, Guildford Dudley, was beheaded on Tower Hill. That same day, the seventeen year-old Lady Jane, who had been imprisoned since Mary's accession, was executed on a specially constructed scaffold on Tower Green. That same week, mysterious phenomena were observed in London—an inverted rainbow, and two suns shining at once—that were taken by some to be an ill-omen.

Less than two weeks later the Duke of Suffolk, Lady Jane's father, was beheaded on Tower Hill. The queen's half-sister, Elizabeth, was implicated in the rebellion, arrested on the advice of Gardiner and imprisoned in the Tower, but escaped the block. As leader of the rebellion, Sir Thomas Wyatt was not so fortunate, suffering a gruesome end on Tower Hill some weeks later.

On 19 March 1554 Hooper was taken from the Fleet to face a commission of bishops and other crown officials. Those present included Gardiner and Bishops Bonner, Day and Tunstall. The principal reason for Hooper's summons was to formally deprive him of his bishoprics, but the meeting quickly degenerated into rowdiness and disorder. Hooper was given little opportunity to defend himself, and whenever he attempted to make a point he was shouted down. It was an altogether unedifying sight. Bishop Day angrily called Hooper a 'hypocrite', Bishop Tunstall and one of the clerks declared him a 'beast', and Justice Morgan verbally abused him at some length. When

asked by Gardiner whether he was married or not—
Gardiner certainly already knew the answer—Hooper
replied assertively, 'Yea, my lord, and will not be unmarried
till death unmarry me'.[103] When Tunstall questioned him
regarding the eucharist—in particular whether he believed
in the real presence of Christ in the sacrament—Hooper
replied that by the authority of God's word there was no
such presence, and consequently he himself did not believe
in such presence. To be a married bishop would have
been enough to deserve deprivation in the new religious
environment, but in denying the real presence Hooper was
declaring himself a heretic; in effect he was also signing
his own death warrant. For the time being the bishops and
officers had heard all they needed to hear, and Hooper
was returned to prison. One week later, papal legate James
Brookes was appointed the new Bishop of Gloucester.

After Easter Hooper was joined in the Fleet by Justice
Sir James Hales, the judge who had resisted signing up to
Edward's Device. He had Protestant sympathies, but it was
his legal probity that had once again got him into trouble.
While the Protestant reforms had still been on the statute
book he had convicted some priests in Kent for celebrating
the Catholic mass. Gardiner had remonstrated with him
for not conforming to the reversion to Catholicism that
had in effect—if not in legal fact—occurred at Mary's
accession, and for not complying with what was clearly the
wish of the queen herself.

Hales was first imprisoned in the King's Bench, then
in the Counter at Bread Street for the whole of Lent,
and finally in the Fleet. On the morning of 12 April he
was visited by Bishop Day of Chichester, and in the

afternoon by Justice Portman, both of whom attempted to dissuade him from his Protestant views. By evening he was clearly depressed and ate little or nothing of his supper. That night he could not sleep, such was his mental turmoil. At 6 o'clock next morning he unsuccessfully attempted suicide, probably with a knife. Hooper was aware of what had happened and Hales' state of mind. He was also aware that Gardiner was immediately trying to use the unhappy episode to discredit 'the true word of God and the professors thereof'. To combat Gardiner's propaganda, Hooper wrote from the Fleet *A Brief Treatise respecting Judge Hales*.[104] Gardiner saw the suicide attempt as an act of desperation by a man who adhered to 'the doctrine of desperation'. Hooper also considered it an act of desperation, but asserted that the cause was Hales' recantation following the pressure exerted by Bishop Day's visit. Hales, he said, had faithfully endured his time in the various prisons:

> till at length by persuasion he waxed weary of the truth, and then denying Christ, that was made man of the substance of the Blessed Virgin Mary, and crediting a false Christ, that was and is made (after the papistical opinion) of bread, was it any marvel [that] the devil entered into this man? ... Therefore it is no marvel [that] such as trust in that false Christ fall into desperation ... It is no marvel therefore to see men that forsake the truth of God to be vexed with evil spirits, and many times to kill themselves. ... So that the papistical doctrine, by this man's example, is a very worm, that biteth the conscience, and never leaveth till it have killed the man that forsaketh the truth, and turned unto lies.

Hales, it seems, finally succumbed to the pressure of the bishops, recanted, and was released from prison. His anguish must have continued, however, because he apparently later drowned himself.

It was a common tactic of the Catholic régime to disseminate rumour and innuendo concerning the Protestant prisoners in an effort to destroy their reputations and to spread discouragement among their followers. Hooper was particularly affronted when he received word that one such slander being circulated was accusing him of being party to treason against the queen herself by writing to 'a godly company' arrested and imprisoned for supposedly treasonable acts. Again, the only way he had of countering such allegations was to make a personal defence in writing, smuggle it out of the Fleet, and have it made public. To this end he wrote *An apology against the untrue and slanderous reports made against me John Hooper, late bishop of Worceter and Gloceter, that I should be a maintainer and encourager of such as cursed the Queen's Majesty's highness,* and attached copies of the letters in question.[105] The letters confirmed that the 'godly company' had been doing nothing more seditious than holding a prayer meeting in a churchyard, and Hooper had done little more than encourage them to persevere in prayer. Moreover, he reminded his readers of the actions he had taken in support of the queen at the time of her accession:

> Seeing in adversity I was with her, and did her service then, I being at liberty, it is falsely and wickedly conspired by the papists that now, she being in real possession of the crown,

and in prosperity, and I a prisoner in captivity, would be against her.

He was convinced of his own innocence and the guilt of his accusers, yet he knew in his heart of hearts that however persuasive his arguments were, he was soon to face death, however it was to be administered: 'Therefore let us rejoice that our time draweth so near to go from this ruinous and decayed city and tabernacle of our bodies: for there is an everlasting mansion in heaven prepared for us.'[106]

11

… these most dangerous times

By April, Anna Hooper and her daughter Rachel had arrived in Frankfurt via Antwerp, and had made arrangements for little Daniel to join them later. It was a very painful time for Anna, separated from the husband she loved, knowing that she would never see him again, and facing the prospect of bringing up their children without him. As much as she could, she comforted herself by prayer and reading the word of God, but she was already grieving. In a letter to Bullinger, dated 20 April 1554, she spoke of carrying 'this burden of widowhood.'[107] As she waited to hear the inevitable news, not knowing if it would arrive that day, the following week or month, or in a year's time, she felt herself numb and in a state of limbo. Correspondence from Bullinger was a huge source of encouragement to her. She explained to her dear friend in Zurich that she habitually read his letters over and over again, 'to add spurs to this dull flesh'.

At the beginning of May, Hooper heard rumours that a number of the Protestant prisoners—including himself—were to be called to a public disputation at Cambridge, similar to the one that Cranmer, Ridley and Hugh Latimer had taken part in at Oxford during the previous month.[108] On 6 May he managed to get a letter to Robert Ferrar, Dr Rowland Taylor, John Bradford, and John Philpot who were all held in the King's Bench in Southwark to alert them to the plans that were afoot and to ensure that they were well prepared for such an event. He urgently sought their advice as to how to respond, and offered his own thoughts. It was a matter to be approached with great caution and wisdom, he felt, particularly as the Oxford disputation had turned out to be something of a stitch-up:

> *Ye know such as shall be censors and judges over us breathe and thirst our blood; and whether we by God's help overcame after the word of God, or by force and subtilty of our adversaries be overcome, this will be the conclusion: our adversaries will say they overcame, as you perceive how they report of those great learned men and godly personages at Oxford.*

Before agreeing to participate, Hooper believed they should stipulate a number of conditions. First, they should have full access to, and use of their theological books, to ensure that they themselves were well briefed and that their adversaries could not get away with making false assertions or taking quotations out of context. Second, they should ensure that honest, sworn notaries were present to make a faithful record of proceedings. Third, if the disputation descended into abuse and disorder, they should immediately appeal to be heard before the queen, Council, or parliament.

Two days later a comprehensive and extensive declaration was drawn up for circulation, signed by Protestant leaders held in Newgate, the Fleet, the King's Bench, and the Marshalsea. It began by following Hooper's advice, setting strict conditions for any participation in a proposed disputation, and then continued with a list of eight fundamental articles of Protestant doctrine and a bold refutation of certain Catholic doctrines and practice. It concluded with a declaration of obedience to the queen and a repudiation of any kind of treason.

As it turned out, despite all this sudden activity and anxiety, the proposed disputation never did happen, but the episode demonstrated the effect of rumour on Hooper and his fellow prisoners.

As summer approached, Hooper was becoming increasingly distressed by his strained communication with the world outside the Fleet and once more felt his life to be 'in very great danger'.[109] Babington was watching him more closely, making it difficult for him to write and send even the briefest note and hindering letters coming in to him. He had not received word from Bullinger for some time, even though Bullinger had in fact continued to write. By the end of the summer, James Haddon, another exiled preacher, writing from Strasbourg, spoke of the 'many ways and means devised' to maintain communication, but still, he reported, Hooper 'almost thinks himself deserted by his friends.'[110]

If good news and encouragement often found it hard to reach Hooper by letter, bad news was able to breach the prison walls all too easily, no doubt with the assistance of the gaolers, particularly if it was something likely to discourage him. He must, therefore, have been told of Philip of Spain's eventual arrival on English shores in the middle of July and the subsequent royal wedding held at Westminster cathedral on 25 July and conducted with full Catholic ceremonial by Gardiner. In sharp contrast to Hooper's dark, meagre existence, the wedding celebrations that continued for several days were full of exuberant singing, dancing, and banqueting.

Hooper no doubt recognised that the Catholic grip on England was tightening, but worse was to come. Following the repeal of the Edwardian reforms, the coercion of some 800 Protestants into exile abroad and the imprisonment of many others, and now a new alliance with Catholic Spain, moves were under way to heal the schism between England and Rome by placing the Church of England once more under the authority of the pope. Pivotal in this aspiration was the return from exile, in November, of Cardinal Reginald Pole.

Pole had Plantagenet blood in his veins through both Edward IV and Richard III, and also through his maternal grandfather, the Duke of Clarence, who had famously drowned in a butt of malmsey wine in the Tower. His mother had been governess to the young Princess Mary and he himself had benefited from an excellent education paid for by Henry VIII. Like Hooper, he had fled abroad during Henry's reign, but his reasons for leaving were very different. He was a staunch Roman Catholic and had vehemently objected to England's break with the papacy and the establishment of the Royal Supremacy in the wake of Henry's need to annul his marriage to Katherine of Aragon. Now, after 20 years he was returning to England as papal legate with the specific aim of accomplishing reunion between England and Rome.

On 12 November Mary's second parliament convened and set about repealing the Act of Attainder that—almost literally—still hung round Pole's neck from the days of his flight. The next day he began his journey back to England, eventually arriving at Westminster on 24 November, just two days after the repeal of the Act against him was given the royal assent. On 28 November he addressed a joint meeting of both houses of parliament and made a formal offer to grant absolution to the realm. His tone was conciliatory rather than censorious: 'My business is not to proceed by way of retrospection, or to question things already settled', he explained: 'As for what passed, it shall be all over-looked and forgotten.'[111]

All that was now required of parliament was to undertake the repeal of all the legislation passed under Henry VIII by which England had broken away from Rome—in particular the Act of Supremacy—and other ecclesiastical legislation passed during the schism. This was duly done, although the contentious issue of the return of secularised church lands and property was put on the back burner. Parliament drew up a document to petition the king and queen to seek the realm's absolution. On 30 November, in a glorious piece of theatre, both houses met again in the presence of the king, queen and papal legate. Gardiner formally presented the petition to Philip and Mary who in turn made a show of discussing the matter with Pole, before the latter announced the absolution.

Two days after England's formal return to papal jurisdiction, Cardinal Pole and the king attended mass at St Paul's, with Bishop Bonner officiating. Stephen Gardiner was asked to preach and rose to the occasion, delivering what was widely considered to be a powerful and perfectly fitting sermon.

The text for that Sunday was 'Now it is time to awake out of sleep', and Gardiner humbly identified himself with a people who had 'slept or rather dreamed' since the schism under Henry VIII. 'I acknowledge my fault,' he declared openly, 'and exhort all who [have] fallen into this sleep through me or with me, with me to awake!'

When he had finished, the huge congregation, numbering over fifteen thousand, knelt down in submission. 'A sight to be seen it was,' observed one of those present, 'and the silence was such that not a cough was heard.' The sermon drew glowing praise from Cardinal Pole, and as the dignitaries exited the church the crowds waiting joyfully outside begged the papal legate for his blessing.

The darkness of the Fleet must have grown even darker for Hooper as news of current events was passed to him. Just when he was in desperate need of encouragement, however, he at last heard from Bullinger. It was clear from this letter, written back at the beginning of October, that Bullinger was aware of the seriousness of Hooper's predicament and wanted to offer what godly comfort he could:

> *Therefore, seeing you have such a large promise, be strong in the Lord, fight a good fight, be faithful unto the end. Consider that Christ, the Son of God, is your captain, and fighteth for you, and that all the prophets, apostles, and martyrs are your fellow-soldiers… Happy are we if we depart in the Lord. May he grant unto you, and to all your fellow-prisoners, faith and constancy.*

Hooper's relief and joy at receiving his dear friend's letter was evident from the brief reply he wrote on 11 December: 'I readily perceived … your ancient feelings of love and affection towards me', he told Bullinger, 'and am most thankful to you that in these most dangerous times you have not forgotten me … They are daily threatening us with death, which we are quite indifferent about; in Christ Jesus we boldly despise the sword and the flames'.[112]

Hooper had not been forgotten, and he himself had not forgotten his family. Recognising that they too needed comforting at this time, he concluded his letter with a plea to Bullinger to write to Anna, 'that most exemplary and godly woman, my wife'.[113]

12

… I consider this life to be death[114]

On Tuesday 22 January 1555 Babington was commanded to take Hooper over the Thames to the Bishop of Winchester's house at St Mary Overie in Southwark to again face the commission led by Gardiner. It was made clear to Hooper that even now the queen's mercy was available to him, if only he would repudiate his Protestant doctrines and return to the Catholic Church by acknowledging the supremacy of the pope. Hooper, however, had come too far to go back now. In the clearest terms he told the commission that he did not consider the pope a true member of Christ's church, let alone head of it. Moreover, he openly claimed that the Catholic church, of which the pope was supposedly head, was itself not the true church of Christ since it was deaf to the voice of Christ. At the same time, he declared, 'If in any point, to me unknown, I have offended the queen's majesty, I shall most humbly submit myself to her mercy, if mercy may be had with safety of conscience, and without the displeasure of God'. He knew of course that mercy would not be his since he had no intention of ignoring his conscience or displeasing God. He was told bluntly that mercy would not be shown by the queen to those who were enemies of the pope. Accordingly, Babington was ordered to return him to the Fleet.

The following Monday 28 January he was again taken before the commission at St Mary Overie, along with along with another Protestant preacher John Rogers who had also faced the commission the previous week. Both men were questioned at length that afternoon; first Hooper and around dusk, Rogers. The prisoners were then held overnight by the compter in Southwark and were neither allowed to speak to one another nor receive visitors.

Next day they appeared yet again before Gardiner and the other commissioners. Seeing that Hooper was not willing to relent, the commission commanded that he be degraded—defrocked—from the priesthood; not from the office of bishop since they refused to recognise the validity of his consecration which had been carried out according to the Protestant Prayer Book of 1549. The order of condemnation pointedly referred to Hooper's early life as a Cistercian monk at Cleeve Abbey in Somerset. Hooper was then led out and Rogers was brought in to be treated in the same way. When the proceedings against the two men were completed they were handed over to the custody of the city sheriffs who took them to the nearby Clink prison.

The Clink[115] was in effect the Bishop of Winchester's private prison, whose inmates were mostly beggars, actors, political enemies of the Bishop, and, particularly, certain of the prostitutes who plied their trade around Southwark. For several centuries until the Reformation the Bishop had acted as a kind of pimp to the local prostitutes—an arrangement sanctioned by a royal licence under Henry II—and the Clink was reserved for any prostitute who dared to work for anyone else or conceal her earnings from the Bishop's officials. The women who 'worked' for the Bishop were known as 'Winchester's geese'; a name that was still used even though Gardiner himself had no such involvement. At the time of Mary's accession a scurrilous report was being spread that the prominent Catholic scholar and clergyman, Dr Hugh Weston, who was unwell with a nasty disease, had been 'smitten with a Winchester goose'.[116]

Hooper's stay in the Clink was very brief. The officials simply wanted to wait for the cover of darkness before transferring him through London's streets to yet another prison, Newgate. Those charged with keeping him secure were taking no chances. Not only did heavily armed guards accompany him, but also sergeants were ordered to go ahead of the party and extinguish the candles of the costermongers who, even at night, sat in the streets to sell their wares. Every attempt was made to keep the transfer as low key as possible so as to avoid any kind of civil disturbance. Even so, Hooper was greeted and encouraged by many people along the way, and responded by asking for their prayers. His probable route took him out of Southwark, over the drawbridge at the southern end of London bridge, across the nineteen wooden piers of the bridge itself, passing through the jumbled collection of buildings that spanned the river, turning left into Cheapside, past St Paul's on his left, and just a little further until he arrived at Newgate prison.

He was to spend the next six days in virtual solitary confinement, expecting execution at any time. His isolation was broken only by daily visits by Bonner and his chaplains who continually attempted to induce him to abjure. Hooper was inclined to refuse to participate in these meetings but agreed to enter into discussions with them to avoid any accusation of pride on the one hand or lack of learning on the other. 'For I fear not their arguments', he declared, 'neither is death terrible unto me'. When he remained steadfast, Bonner sought to discredit him by the usual tactic of rumour spreading; this time word went out that the former Bishop of Gloucester had indeed recanted. When Hooper came to hear what was being said about him, he was particularly grieved to learn that a number of his supporters had succumbed to the Bishop of London's malicious lies. 'Truly this report of weak brethren is a double trouble and a triple cross',[117] he lamented in an open letter dated 2 February. He also struck a defiant note:

> For I have hitherto left all things of this world, and suffered great pains and long imprisonment; and I thank God I am ready even as gladly to suffer death for the truth I have preached as a mortal man may be … I have taught this truth with my tongue and pen heretofore, and hereafter shortly will confirm by God's grace the same with my blood.

On Monday 4 February Hooper and Rogers were taken to the prison chapel where Bonner was waiting with a number of witnesses and a notary to keep a written record of proceedings. Bonner had arrived to carry out the degrading pronounced by the commission on the previous Tuesday. The procedure followed the usual pattern of first dressing the prisoner in the full attire of a priest and then symbolically removing each item until only the final undergarment remained. Hooper was then returned to his cell to await his fate. Rogers, however, once degraded, was ordered to be taken immediately to Smithfield to be burned. Bonner personally turned down his request for one final meeting with his wife before facing the fire. As it happened, this vindictiveness was thwarted because Rogers did in fact get to see his wife and eleven children in the street as he was escorted to Smithfield. Even that sight, and the customary last-minute offer of the queen's pardon could not shake Rogers' resolve or composure, and he became the first Protestant martyr of Mary's reign.

Hooper had heard with great joy that he was to return to Gloucester for execution, and so prepared for the journey in good heart. At around 4 o'clock next morning his bed and person were searched for letters or notes, and then he was taken to a place near St Dunstan's church in Fleet Street where he was handed over to six horse guards who were charged with escorting him back to Gloucester. As a physical sign of their authority, the London sheriffs handed the guards a small brass mace with the coat of arms of Philip and Mary at one end and that of the city of London at the other. Under the cover of darkness the guards took their prisoner to the *Angel* hostelry where Hooper had an unusually hearty breakfast, after which the party set off on horseback as dawn was breaking. Over the next three days they stopped to rest at the places Hooper had been accustomed to frequent on his numerous journeys over the same route in the past four years.

By late afternoon on Thursday 7 February, having lunched at Cirencester, the party arrived at the escarpment overlooking Gloucester. Hooper must have had mixed feelings as he gazed towards the city where he had worked so hard as shepherd of his flock; a sense of coming home after his many months of imprisonment in London, yet a realisation of his inevitable and impending death. As the party descended the hill and came within a mile of the city they were met by crowds of local people who, having heard of their former bishop's approach, had come out in the dusk to see him pass by. The mood of those who stood watching was sombre, and although there was no real threat of disorder, the sheer number of people caused concern among Hooper's guards who feared an attempt might be made to release their prisoner. One of the guards urgently rode on ahead into the city to seek assistance from the mayor and sheriffs, who responded by ordering the people to stay indoors and by sending some armed men to the north gate of the city to meet Hooper's party as it entered Gloucester.

By now it was dark and Hooper was taken to spend the night under guard at the house of Robert and Agnes Ingram opposite St Nicholas' church in the western part of the city. No doubt he was physically exhausted by the journey, and the sciatica that had developed during his time in prison had been aggravated by three days on horseback. He quietly ate supper and then retired to sleep for some time before spending the night in prayer. All the

while a close watch was kept on him, but when morning
came he was permitted to go alone into an adjoining room
to spend his last full day in private prayer, breaking off only
to eat and to receive a number of visitors.

One of those who came to see him that day was Sir
Anthony Kingston[118] who, following his unpleasant and
costly dealings with his then bishop at the Consistory
court, had later become a convinced Protestant through
Hooper's teaching. He came, not only as one of those
'of reputation' who had been appointed to witness the
execution, but as a friend. When he was brought into
Hooper's quiet room and saw him praying, this battle-
hardened soldier was moved to tears. Strangely, Hooper
did not recognise his visitor at first; perhaps he had been
so deep in prayer, communing with his Lord, that even
if his wife Anna had walked into the room just then
it would have taken him a moment or two to register
who she was, or perhaps his visitor's sudden grief had
become a temporary disguise. In any case, Kingston
respectfully yet familiarly introduced himself and Hooper
immediately responded with recognition. The two men
exchanged pleasantries before Kingston—out of affection,
not malice—tried to persuade his old friend, even at this
eleventh hour, to accept the queen's mercy, saying, 'But
alas! consider this life sweet, and death is bitter. Therefore,
seeing life may be had, desire to live; for life hereafter may
do good'. This was not arm-twisting or sly psychological
games; it was a simple human plea for Hooper to save his
life.

Hooper graciously thanked Kingston for his well-
meaning advice but replied:

True it is master Kingston, that death is bitter, and life is sweet: but, alas! consider that the death to come is more bitter, and the life to come is more sweet. Therefore, for the desire and love I have for the one, and the terror and fear of the other, I do not so much regard this death, nor esteem this life, but have settled myself, through the strength of God's Holy spirit, patiently to pass through the torments and extremities of the fire now prepared for me, rather than to deny the truth of his word, desiring you and others, in the meantime, to commend me to God's mercy in your prayers.

Hooper's mind was made up, and nothing Kingston might say could shake his determination. Kingston again expressed his heartfelt gratitude to the former bishop, and as they said their farewells he again wept. At that moment Hooper's composure finally broke, and as the two men parted, his face, which had once been struck in anger, was streaked with tears of profound sadness.

Kingston himself was soon to be imprisoned briefly in the Tower for being obstructive in the House of Commons in opposition to the queen and her Council. In just over a year he was to die in mysterious circumstances near Cirencester while under arrest following a failed plot to replace Mary with her sister Elizabeth.

Later that afternoon Hooper had a quite different visitor. Thomas Drowry was a blind boy who had recently been imprisoned for maintaining Protestant beliefs. He had heard of Hooper's arrival back in Gloucester and was desperate to meet with him. He pleaded with his gaolers and was eventually granted his wish. The two talked, and as Hooper heard the boy's testimony he was moved with godly pride and fatherly affection. 'Ah, poor boy!' he said, 'God hath taken from thee thy outward sight, for what reason he best knoweth: but he hath given thee another sight much more precious, for he hath endued thy soul with the eyes of knowledge and faith. God give thee grace continually to pray unto him, that thou lose not that sight, for then shouldest thou be blind both in body and soul'.

Young Thomas was to remain imprisoned for more than a year after this encounter and was finally burned at Gloucester on 15 May 1556, along with Thomas Croker, a bricklayer.

A staunch Catholic who was known to Hooper also came to see him to express sadness at the former bishop's plight. Hooper's response to him was typically forthright: 'Be sorry for thyself, man', he said, 'and lament thine own wickedness; for I am well, I thank God, and death to me for Christ's sake is welcome'.

That evening the mayor of Gloucester, Thomas Bell junior, arrived at Ingram's house, accompanied by the town sheriffs, William Jenkins and William Bond, and the aldermen of the city. They greeted their former bishop cordially and respectfully. Hooper was gladdened by their friendliness. Addressing Bell, he said:

> *Master mayor, I give most hearty thanks to you, and to the rest of your brethren, that you have vouchsafed to take me, a prisoner and a condemned man, by the hand; whereby, to my rejoicing, it is apparent that your old love and friendship towards me is not altogether extinguished; and I trust also that all those things are not utterly forgotten which, as your*

bishop and pastor appointed by the late godly king, I taught you in times past.

He expressed himself fully submitted to the sheriffs who were charged with the practicalities of his execution, asking just one thing of them, 'that there might be a quick fire'. Sadly, they were to fail utterly to fulfil this humble request.

Like Kingston, many of those in the civic party were deeply saddened by their meeting with Hooper. Jenkins and Bond were perhaps less moved, being well aware of their solemn responsibilities. When the guards who had brought the prisoner from London handed him over to the local officials—exchanging the mace at the same time—the Gloucester sheriffs wanted to move him out of Ingram's house and into the gaol above the north gate. This would have happened had it not been for the intervention of Hooper's guards themselves. Having experienced first-hand his gentleness and co-operation over the previous days and nights they managed to persuade the sheriffs to allow him to remain at Ingram's house, saying that even a child would be able to guard such a compliant prisoner, and they themselves would rather continue to watch him than see him spend his last night in the squalor and indignity of the common gaol. Hooper's final words to his visitors were that he faced death 'a faithful servant of God and a true and obedient subject to the queen'.

It had been an emotionally draining day for him. He retired to bed to rest at 5 o'clock and, as he had done the previous evening, he slept for a while to prepare himself for spending the night in prayer. Some time during his travail a certain poem came into his mind[119] and he was no doubt reminded of the advice he once gave his friend William Cecil. He took a lump of coal and wrote the words onto a wall in his room:

> *Content thyself with patience*
> *With Christ to bear the cross of pain,*
> *Who can or will recompense*
> *A thousand-fold with joys again.*
> *Let nothing cause thy heart to fail;*
> *Launch out thy boat, hoise up thy sail,*
> *Put from the shore;*
> *And be thou sure thou shalt attain*
> *Unto the port that shall remain*
> *For evermore.*
> *Fear not death, pass not for bands,*
> *Only in God put thy whole trust;*
> *For he will require thy blood at their hands;*
> *And thou dost know that once die thou must:*
> *Only for that thy life if thou give,*
> *Death is no death, but a means for to live.*
> *Do not despair:*
> *Of no worldly tyrant see thou dread;*
> *Thy compass, which is God's word, shall thee lead,*
> *And the wind is fair.*[120]

When morning finally arrived, Hooper wanted to be left alone right up to the last possible moment and asked that no visitors be allowed to disturb him.

In a funeral sermon preached at Zurich in 1549, shortly before he returned to England, Hooper had declared:

In the hour of death is like to be our hardest assault and greatest danger. The book of our conscience shall be opened. The devil will aggravate and give all the strengh he can to our sin, and will (if God suffer him) either extenuate and diminish the mercy of God, or clean cause us to despair: hell then will gape and open his mouth upon us.[121]

The response to such trials, he had said, was to be assured by the word of God and to trust God's promise that 'Blessed are they that die in the Lord' (Revelation 14). Now, in these final solitary moments he was surely sustained by that same conviction.

At 8 o'clock—an hour before the appointed time—the official commissioners overseeing the execution arrived at the house. They were fully aware of their solemn duty, having received the queen's order that read:

Whereas, JOHN HOOPER, *who of late was called Bishop of Worcester and Gloucester, is by due order of the laws ecclesiastic, condemned and judged for a most obstinate, false, detestable heretic, and committed to our secular power, to be burned according to the wholesome and good laws of our realm, in that case provided, forasmuch as, in those cities and dioceses, thereof he hath in times past preached and taught most pestilent heresies and doctrine to our subjects there; we have therefore given order, that the said* HOOPER, *who yet persisteth obstinate, and hath refused mercy when it was graciously offered, shall be put to execution, in the said city of Gloucester, for the example and terror there. And will that you calling unto you some of reputation dwelling in the shire, such as ye think best, shall repair unto our said city, and be at the said execution, assisting our mayor and sheriffs of the same city in his behalf; and forasmuch also as the said* HOOPER *is, as heretics be, a vain glorious person and delighteth in his tongue, and having liberty may use his said tongue to persuade such as he hath seduced to persist in the miserable opinion that he hath sown amongst them, our pleasure is therefore, and we require you to take order that the said* HOOPER *be neither at the time of his execution, nor in going to the place thereof, suffered to speak at large, but thither to be led quietly, and in silence, for eschewing of further infection, and such inconveniency, as may otherwise ensure in this part. Whereof fail you not, as ye tender our pleasure.*[122]

These men 'of reputation dwelling in the shire' included, amongst others, Sir Anthony Kingston, Mayor Bell junior, his father former mayor Sir Thomas Bell, Sir John Brydges—recently created Lord Chandos of Sudeley—Sir George Herbert representing the Worcester diocese and member of the Council for the Welsh Marches, and Lord Henry Berkeley who, on hearing of the Wyatt rebellion, had armed five hundred of his tenants and was heading to London in support of Mary when Wyatt was arrested. While these men waited, they shared wine provided at the mayor's command and a cost of five shillings and eight pence to the city's coffers, and Hooper's request not to be disturbed was respected.

When the sheriffs went to bring Hooper down from his room they were accompanied by a group of heavily armed men; they were clearly still anxious to secure and protect their prisoner and leave nothing to chance. Hooper, however, was taken aback by what seemed to him an unduly heavy-handed approach. 'Mister Sheriffs', he said, 'I am no traitor, neither need you to have made such preparation to bring me to the place where I must suffer; for if ye had desired me, I would have gone alone to the stake, and have troubled none of you all'.

He borrowed a gown from Robert Ingram, put on a hat and, steadying himself with a staff, stepped outside into a chilly morning to make the short walk to the place set aside for his execution. Immediately he was struck by the huge crowd that had gathered in the city. There were perhaps as many as seven thousand people—many more than the city's own population. Saturday being one of the two market days at Gloucester (the other being Wednesday) the place was full of buyers and sellers from the surrounding area, as well as the locals. Many would have come especially to see the execution; his adversaries from Worcester may well have been among the crowd. No doubt people were there for all kinds of reasons, from morbid curiosity and hatred, through detached curiosity, to affection for a still revered and loved pastor.

The place of execution was on raised ground near a great elm tree, a stone's throw from the church of St Mary de Lode, and outside the thirteenth-century St Mary's Gate, the western entrance into the cathedral precincts. The site was not chosen by chance. Not only was it tantalisingly close to the former bishop's seat, but also it was directly overlooked by the windows of the college of priests above the gate, where he used to teach the students his 'pestilent heresies'. As he was brought to the prepared stake, some of those watching were surprised to see him smiling—he was a man more known for his severe appearance than for his smile. Every vantage point was taken; people filled every window of the houses and perched among the boughs of the surrounding trees.

The crowds probably expected Hooper to address them, but as always he submitted himself to the conditions placed on him. As he prepared for execution he would not even stand and pray out loud but rather knelt down to do so quietly. However, seeing a friendly face in the crowd he insistently beckoned someone to come closer to hear his final prayer.[123] This friend was Edmund Brydges, grandson of Lord Chandos. He heeded Hooper's request and stepped out of the crowd.

Hooper began to pray through the Apostles' Creed but was soon interrupted when a man stepped forward and produced a box which he placed on a stool next to him, saying it contained a pardon from the queen which could be his if only he confessed the error of his ways. The box may or may not have held such a document, but either way Hooper was not to be tempted, and twice pleaded, 'If you love my soul away with it!'

The box was therefore taken away and Lord Chandos responded to Hooper's defiance by declaring, 'Seeing there is no remedy, despatch him quickly'. Hooper, however, asked to be permitted to complete his prayer, and Lord Chandos agreed, but made it clear to his grandson—who was still beside Hooper—that the prayer must not be used as a cloak for anything else; if the prisoner abused the opportunity he would be executed without delay.

Hooper continued:

> O Lord Jesus, that for whose love I leave willingly this life,

and desire the bitter death of the cross with the loss of all my worldly things, than either to abide the blasphemy of thy most holy name, or to obey unto men in breaking of thy commandments; thou seest, Lord, that where I might live in wealth to worship a false god, and to honour thine enemy, I choose rather the torments of my body, and the loss of this my life, and have counted all things but vile dust and dung, that I might win thee; which death is more dear unto me than thousands of gold and silver: such love, Lord, hast thou laid up in my breast, that I hunger for thee as the deer that is wounded desireth the soil ... Accept this burnt sacrifice, O heavenly Father, not for the sacrifice's sake, but for thy dear Son's sake my Saviour; for whose testimony I offer this my free-will offering with all my heart, with all my strength, with all my soul ...

In all Hooper was permitted to pray for half an hour without further interruption before concluding with the words: 'O Lord, into thy hands I commend my spirit; thou hast redeemed me, O God of truth. Lord, have mercy upon me; Christ, have mercy upon me; Lord, have mercy upon me. Amen.'

Once he had finished, the sheriffs wasted no time in preparing him for the stake. He removed the gown that he had borrowed and asked that it might be returned to its owner. He wanted to keep the rest of his outer-garments on but the sheriffs would not allow him to do so. He patiently stood there while his doublet, hose, and under-jacket were removed, leaving him in just a shirt, which he tucked between his legs. As was to be common practice at the burnings under Mary, the guards placed a bladder of gunpowder under each arm and between his legs. This was intended as an act of mercy, to shorten the time of suffering by hastening death. The fact that Nicholas Ridley and Hugh Latimer, who later suffered similarly at Oxford, accepted gunpowder was used by at least one Catholic divine to prove that they were not true martyrs since they desired such a speedy release.

Hooper stood up on the stool on which the queen's pardon had supposedly been placed, and asked those watching to pray for him and join him in saying the Lord's Prayer. The sheriffs wanted to fasten him to the stake with three strong iron bands, to be put round his neck, waist, and legs, but Hooper declared himself confident that God's strength would enable him to withstand the flames without flinching, falling or fainting. Accordingly, it was agreed that he would only be fastened round his waist. Unfortunately, the iron brought for the purpose had been made a little too short and Hooper, whose stomach had swollen due to the privations of his imprisonment, had to physically hold himself in so that the iron could be fastened tightly around his body and the stake.

At that point the executioner stepped forward and, as was the custom, asked forgiveness of the one to be burned. Even now Hooper was gracious, assuring the man that he had done nothing that required the former bishop's forgiveness. The man insisted, saying, 'Oh, sir, I am appointed to make the fire', as if he imagined Hooper did not know who he was and why he was there. 'Thou dost not offend me', replied Hooper gently. 'God forgive thee thy sins, and do thine office. I pray thee'.

The man duly prepared for the order to light the fire.

Reeds were brought and Hooper himself directed their placement around the stake and placed a bundle with the gunpowder under each arm. Along with the reeds there were two horse-loads of faggots that, being green rather than dry and seasoned, took some time to kindle once the fire had been lit. When the flames began to rise around Hooper, the strong wind blew them away from the stake and left him only mildly burned.

Having used up the supply of reeds, and realising the unsuitability of the green faggots, a small number of dry faggots was brought and placed around the stake. Another fire was kindled, but this second attempt was hardly more effective than the first. The flames again battled with the wind and mostly burned Hooper's lower body, singed his hair, and lightly scorched his skin. As he wiped his eyes, he cried out, 'For God's love, good people, let me have more fire!'

Sadly, he was not to be granted his 'quick fire', but was destined to have his suffering cruelly drawn out.

A third attempt resulted in a stronger fire, yet his agony continued. The bladders of gunpowder finally broke open but failed to explode as hoped. Given that the city authorities had already demonstrated a degree of incompetence in supplying green faggots in the first place, and too small a quantity of both reeds and seasoned faggots, the gunpowder was probably either second-rate or damp.

After more than three-quarters of an hour in the flames, Hooper summoned his strength one last time to cry out a final prayer: 'Lord Jesus, have mercy upon me! Lord Jesus, have mercy upon me! Lord Jesus, receive my spirit'.

Finally, as the flames strengthened, Hooper's body underwent gruesome disfigurement. His mouth blackened, his tongue swelled, and his lips shrank to the gums. One arm fell into the fire, and the fingers on his remaining hand dripped with water, fat and blood. As the fire was stoked he wavered from the stake for the first time and, bowing forwards, breathed his last. In the end, it was said, he died as quietly as a child in his bed.

While the city officials seemed to have tried to save money concerning the fuel for the fire, little expense was spared in terms of reward and hospitality for those involved.[124] The six guards who had escorted Hooper from London received forty shillings between them. A sergeant from Tewkesbury was rewarded with the sum of five shillings and seven pence for bringing the Queen's pardon. The Bishop of Gloucester, James Brookes, received a gift of bread, wine, figs, almonds, sugar and other delicacies to mark the occasion. By the commandment of the mayor, the city paid for wine and fine sugar for Lord Stafford and Lord Berkeley at the home of the mayor's father. That evening a dinner was held at the mayor's home, paid for by the city and attended by Lord Chandos and others who had officiated at the execution that morning.

Anna Hooper had long been expecting the worst, but when the news finally reached her she was heartbroken. Writing from Frankfurt on 11 April 1555 she pleaded with her old and precious friend Bullinger: 'I pray you therefore by the holy friendship of the most holy martyr my husband, of whom being now deprived I consider this life to be death, do not forsake me.'[125] Enclosed with the letter was an English coin, sent by her daughter Rachel, showing

Philip and Mary—or as Anna described them—Ahab and
Jezebel.[126]

13

… more fair and durable than stone[127]

According to Rev. H.C. Minchin, vicar of St Mary de Lode, Monday 9 February 1863 was more like a day in May; the *Gloucester Journal* reported that 'the air was soft and balmy, and floods of bright sunshine poured down into the streets'. How different from that chilly day three hundred and eight years before when people from Gloucester and beyond had gathered to witness the burning of Bishop Hooper. Now the city prepared to celebrate the inauguration of the Hooper Memorial.

Without the involvement of masonic lodges it was perhaps a less flamboyant event than the laying of the foundation stone a year and a half earlier. What it lacked in pageantry, however, it more than made up for in terms of sheer public excitement. The procession that departed the Tolsey at half past two that afternoon consisted of Mayor Nicks in his scarlet and fur, local schoolboys enjoying an afternoon away from classroom lessons, various civic dignitaries, local clergy, and members of the Memorial Committee, all being led by the band of the Artillery and Engineer Corps in their white uniforms, playing a solemn march. As before, the pavements were crowded, windows were filled with spectators, and hundreds of people followed on behind as the procession made its way down Westgate Street, past the cathedral that seemed to glow red in the afternoon sun, along Three Cocks Lane, and into St Mary's Square for a brief service at the old church of St Mary de Lode.

When the congregation spilled out into the Square once more, it was greeted by a huge, boisterous crowd waiting somewhat impatiently for the unveiling of the statue. Again, every vantage point around the Square was occupied, and the old college of priests above St Mary's gateway was 'filled with an animated company of the fair sex'.

The monument was very grand. Constructed in the previous year by local builder Oliver Estcourt and local architects Medland and Maberly at a cost of four hundred pounds—raised by public subscription—it stood forty-five feet high and consisted of three steps and a pedestal of Murrel Down stone, supporting a large, highly ornate canopy containing the still veiled statue, and above it an intricately crafted spire—both of local Forest stone. On a brass plate on one side of the square pedestal was an inscription recording the fact that the monument stood on the site of an earlier, far more modest monument given by James Clealand of Bangor, Ireland in 1826. On the opposite side, engraved into a second brass plate, was a particularly fitting inscription:

Gloria Soli Deo
"For the witness of Jesus and for the Word of God"
"not accepting deliverance,"
John Hooper, D.D. Bishop of Gloucester and Worcester,
was burnt to ashes on this spot, February 9, Anno Domini 1555.

At the invitation of Rev. Minchin, the Mayor stepped forward and, after a few words of reflection, removed the muslin sheet covering the statue.

The revealed figure was the work of E.W. Thornhill of Dublin, and the design had been chosen through a competition. Sculpted from a single, perfect block of Portland stone, it stood eight feet tall and managed to capture its subject's grim severity; all the more imposing for being set up on the pedestal, as if standing in a pulpit over a congregation. Here was Hooper the preacher, facing the windows of the old college of priests, and with his right hand raised in exhortation and his left hand gripping a Bible. The cost of the statue—one hundred guineas—had again been raised by public subscription. Ironically Hooper was depicted wearing the vestments against which he had fought so hard.

The ceremony drew to a close with a hymn after which Rev. Minchin dutifully pronounced the benediction.

At five o'clock that evening, around fifty of those involved in the inauguration assembled at the King's Head Hotel and enjoyed an excellent dinner. Recalling that the civic dignitaries present at Hooper's burning had also afterwards sat down to dinner, Mayor Nicks reflected that on that occasion 'the Mayor and corporation, after the execution of so good a man, should rather have gone home to weep than have gone to dine together'. However, he continued, 'dining was so much a custom with Englishmen that nothing could be done without a dinner'.

The following weekend the *Journal* printed a poem entitled *The Veiled Martyr*, written especially to mark the inauguration. One verse in particular seemed to grasp the fact that even the finest monument could never really do justice to the extraordinary life and death of such a remarkable man:

> *Three centuries have passed, since in the car*
> *Of fire, his foes provided, he to Heaven*
> *Passed with abundant entrance. We have met,*
> *And with a tardy justice, now have given*
> *Expression to his memory's worthiness,*
> *In sculptured monument, from quarry riven:*
> *He needs it not; his name and deeds alone*
> *Are monument more fair and durable than stone.*

Bibliography

Primary Sources

Calendar of State Papers Domestic—Edward VI 1547–1553 ed. CS Knighton, HMSO London 1992

Early Writings of John Hooper ed. Rev. Samuel Carr The Parker Society, Cambridge University Press 1843

Later Writings of Bishop Hooper ed. Rev. Charles Nevinson The Parker Society, Cambridge University Press 1852

Original Letters Relative to the English Reformation 2 vols ed. H. Christmas, The Parker Society 1856

The Acts and Monuments of John Foxe vols V & VI ed. Rev. G. Townsend 1846

Gloucester Journal and *Gloucester Chronicle* Gloucester Local Studies Library

Secondary Sources

Alford, Stephen *Kingship and Politics in the reign of Edward VI* Cambridge University Press Cambridge 2002

Davenport, James *Notes on the Bishopric of Worcester 1547–1559* Gloucestershire Collection Worcester 1916

Hockaday, F.S. *Gloucester Consistory Court* Transactions of the Bristol & Gloucestershire Archaeological Society vol. XLVI

Hunt E.W. *The Life and Times of John Hooper, Bishop of Gloucester* Edwin Mellen Lampeter 1992

Litzenberger, Caroline *Responses of the laity to changes in official religious policy in Gloucestershire (1541–1580)* D.Phil Dissertation Trinity College Cambridge 1993 (Gloucestershire Records Office)

Loades, D.M. *The Oxford Martyrs* B.T. Batsford London 1970

Loades, David *The Reign of Mary Tudor* 2nd ed. Longman London & New York 1991

Loades, David *The Mid-Tudor Crisis, 1545–1565* Macmillan London 1992

MacCulloch, Diarmaid *The Later Reformation in England 1547–1603* Macmillan Basingstoke 1990

MacCulloch, Diarmaid *Thomas Cranmer—A Life* Yale University Press London 1996

Muller, J.A. *The Letters of Stephen Gardiner* Greenwood Press Connecticut U.S.A. 1970

Parker, T.H.L. *English Reformers* vol XXVI Library of Christian Classics, S.C.M. Press London 1966

Porter, Roy *London* Hamish Hamilton London 1994

Price, F. Douglas *Gloucester Diocese Under Bishop Hooper 1551–3* Transactions of the Bristol & Gloucestershire Archaeological Society vol. LX

Price, FD *The Administration of the Diocese of Gloucester 1547–1579* BA Thesis 2 vols 1939 (Gloucestershire Records Office)

Primus, John H. *The Vestments Controversy* 1960

Ridley, Jasper *Bloody Mary's Martyrs* Constable London 2001

Sheppard, Francis *London—A History* Oxford University Press Oxford 1998

Starkey, David *Elizabeth* Vintage London 2001

Strype John *Ecclesiastical Memorials* (3 vols in 6) Clarendon Press London 1822

Tittler, Robert *The Reign of Mary I* 2nd ed. Seminar Studies in History Longman London & New York 1991

Weir, Alison *The Six Wives of Henry VIII* Pimlico London 1991

Endnotes

Chapter 1

1. Foxe vol. VI. p. 638.
2. *Later Writings* pp. ix, x.
3. *Original Letters* p. 350.
4. OL p. 49.
5. OL p. 50.
6. OL pp. 51, 52.
7. OL p. 63.
8. Quoted in Loades, *Oxford Martyrs* p. 59.
9. For Gardiner's opposition to change during the king's minority see Muller, and Loades, OM p. 55.
10. Foxe vol. VI p. 637.
11. *A Detection of the Devil's Sophistrie* see *Early Writings* pp. 99,100.
12. EW p. 101.
13. EW p. 117.
14. Foxe vol. VI p. 639.
15. LW p. x ; Strype 2.1 pp. 66, 68.
16. For Edward Underhill see Strype 2.1 pp. 176–183; 3.1 pp. 92–102.
17. OL, p. 34.

Chapter 2

18. Proceedings related in this chapter are from Foxe vol. V. pp. 741–800.

19. OL, p. 558.

20. OL p. 70.

Chapter 3

21. OL p. 69.

22. *A Declaration of the ten holy commandments ...* is in EW.

23. OL p. 71.

24. For Hooper's cordial relations with Cranmer see OL p. 71.

25. OL p. 76.

26. OL p. 82.

27. OL p. 76.

28. For Hooper's remarks on his daughter see OL p. 74.

29. The text of the Lenten sermons is in EW.

30. EW p. 35.

31. OL p. 81.

32. OL p. 79.

33. For Gardiner's imprisonment and trial see Muller p. xxxi.

Chapter 4

34. A detailed discussion of the Vestments Controversy is in Primus.

35. Foxe.

36. OL p. 79.

37. OL p. 487.

38. For the establishment of the Strangers Church see *Calendar of State Papers Domestic—Edward VI* pp. 166, 167.

39. Second imprint of *the ten holy commandments* in EW.

40. For Hooper's accusation against Ridley, and Ridley's accusation against Hooper see MacCulloch p. 15.

41. For John à Lasco's letter to the king see Strype 2.2 pp. 34–36.

42. Quoted in Primus p. 36.
43. OL p. 487.
44. Quoted in Primus p. 46.
45. OL p. 86.
46. OL p. 673.
47. The text of *A godly Confession* ... is in LW.
48. OL p. 487.
49. For the Fleet prison see Porter p. 175.
50. Quoted in Primus p. 62.
51. For Hooper's attire see Foxe vol.VI. p. 641; OL p. 271 note.
52. OL p. 187.
53. My modernised version of the original Oath quoted in Price *Gloucester Diocese Under Bishop Hooper* pp. 53, 54.

Chapter 5
54. LW p. xvii.
55. The Pastoral Letter, Articles, Injunctions, Interrogatories and Demands are in LW.
56. Results of the visitation are in LW p. 151.
57. The case of William Phelps is in LW pp. 152–154.
58. The case of John Wynter is in LW pp. 155, 156.
59. The *Godly and most necessary Annotations* ... are in LW.
60. For Guy Eton, John Parkhurst and John Rastell see CSPD Edward VI p. 196; Strype 2.1 p. 325.
61. Foxe vol. VI p. 643.
62. CSPD Edward VI SP 10/3, 13.

Chapter 6
63. For John à Lasco's wife and Cranmer's chaplain see MacCulloch *Thomas Cranmer* pp. 483, 487.
64. OL p. 94.

65. The text of *An Homily to be read ...* is in LW.

66. Background to the Sweating sickness is in Weir p. 97.

67. LW p. xxi.

68. OL p. 441.

69. OL p. 442.

70. For Hooper and parliament see LW p. 59 note.

71. For details of the Canon Law commission see OL p. 580.

Chapter 7

72. Background to this chapter is in Davenport *Notes on the Bishopric of Worcester 1547–1559.*

73. OL pp. 494, 500.

74. OL p. 580.

75. OL p. 23.

76. LW p. xviii.

77. LW p. xviii.

78. LW p. xix.

79. LW p. xix.

80. Foxe vol.VI. p. 644.

Chapter 8

81. For details of the royal succession see Starkey p. 115.

82. OL p. 593.

83. Lord Audley to William Cecil in CSPD Edward VI p. 294.

84. OL p. 365.

85. Quoted in Tittler p. 83.

86. LW p. 557.

87. OL p. 100.

Chapter 9

88. The place and date of Hooper's marriage is suggested by Hunt.

89. For the role of Protestant fishermen see Ridley p. 52.

90. LW p.xxii.

91. OL pp. 53, 54.

92. Hooper's letter of 7 January 1554.

93. OL p. 100.

94. OL p. 741.

95. For Mary's coronation see Tittler pp. 84, 85.

96. For the papal envoys see Loades *The Reign of Mary Tudor* p. 104.

97. Bullinger to Calvin OL p. 742.

98. Hooper in the Fleet LW pp. 620, 621.

99. OL p. 103.

100. Various letters from prison are in LW.

101. Ridley's letter is in OL p. 486 note; Foxe vol. VI. pp. 642, 643.

Chapter 10

102. Quoted in Loades RMT p. 57.

103. Foxe vol.VI p. 646.

104. *A Brief Treatise respecting Judge Hales* is in LW.

105. *An apology against the untrue …* is in LW.

106. LW p. 567.

Chapter 11

107. Anna Hooper to Bullinger OL pp. 110, 111.

108. For details of the proposed Cambridge disputation see LW.

109. OL p. 104.

110. OL p. 293.

111. Quoted in Tittler p. 90.

112. OL p. 104.

113. OL p. 105.

Chapter 12

114. The background to this chapter is based on Foxe's account.

115. For details of the Clink see Porter p. 56.

116. Strype 3.1 p. 31.

117. LW p. 622.

118. Sir Anthony Kingston see Starkey pp.190–193; for a fuller account see also DM Loades *Two Tudor Conspiracies* (Cambridge 1965).

119. The origin of this poem is suggested by Ridley pp. 171, 172.

120. The poem is given in LW p.xxx; 'a means' in line 16 is 'amens' in the original.

121. The text of the funeral sermon, preached on January 13 1549 is given in EW.

122. My modernised version of the original order for execution given in Document SV 9.3 Glos. Collection.

123. Hooper's prayer is given in LW pp. xxix, xxx.

124. Civic expenses are given in the Athenaeum extract 20 April 1878 in the Glos. Collection.

125. OL p. 114.

126. Rachel's coin is mentioned in OL p. 115.

Chapter 13

127. This chapter is based on the account of the ceremony in the Gloucester *Journal* of 14 February, 1863, and other details from documents in the Glos. Collection.

A 'Hooper Trail'

—places to visit relating to Hooper

Gloucester Cathedral.

Gloucester Folk Museum, Westgate Street, which is traditionally known as "Bishop Hooper's Lodging" and contains a number of items relating to Hooper, including the mace and an intriguing portion of charred stake discovered some years ago in St Mary's Square!

The Hooper Memorial, St Mary's Square.

The College of Priests, St Mary's Square, overlooking the Memorial.

Blackfriars, off Westgate Street, which was the home of Sir Thomas Bell who attended Hooper's burning.

Cleeve Abbey, north Somerset (owned by English Heritage) where Hooper is thought to have lived as a Cistercian monk.

Index